Author's picture: Jean-Paul Loyer
Cover design: Betty Massion— Les GermanCreative
Graphic Design: David Breysse
Printer: Lulu.com

All rights reserved in all countries
ISBN 978-0-244-12350-5
Legal deposit: October 2018
CDC France
430 Clos de la Courtine
93160 Noisy-Le-Grand

12 days

The inspiring story of an entrepreneur who spent 12 days alone without food or water creating a method to make you rich, happy and proud of yourself.

ERIC BEHANZIN

Contents

TESTIMONIALS

"If you want better answers, find better questions! This sentence sums up Eric's philosophy and exceptional talent.
He has the enviable ability to reveal yourself to you by means of wise questioning. He helps you reconnect with what drives you, and gives you the action plan to make it all happen remarkably.
His conviction and clarity are striking.
His enthusiasm is wonderfully contagious.
You finally know who you are (conviction) and where you are going (clarity)... And that's a game changer!"

David Breysse
Author of "Words that make millions"
and Founder of "T!LT" Academy

"I was lucky enough to meet Eric and now my life has found new meaning... I can definitely say that with Eric's help, obvious things I hadn't been able to see before suddenly were made clear. He is gifted with double vision; he knows how to look at what is, and what is yet to come. A way of seeing the future!
There are many things that we hide from ourselves, or things our subconscious doesn't want to see. Talking to Eric is like standing in front of a three-dimensional mirror, with depth and height.
I am so grateful for this man's talent, he sees beyond what meets the eyes, to the inner, greater self, which cannot be seen from the inside. That is why you need a mirror.
He is a mirror that provides a very powerful reflection. I recommend him to everyone, especially to those with ambition. Thank you, Eric."

Jean Sommer
Public Speaking Expert

"After years spent being coached by Eric, whether for my career or to enhance my personal development, I'm still impressed by his ability to bounce back and transform a difficult situation into one of life's treasure. He is always ready to commit himself humanely and completely, to help you make your dreams come true."

Beehann, Actress and Singer
(The Voice France season 5, Dirty Dancing : the musical, etc.)

"I have over 20 years of personal development experience. I have been trained in NPL and MBTI, I've had coaches, and many different mentors. Eric is the only one who, in record time, was able to put his finger on two key elements of my personality that turned my brain upside down. Most coaches work on the What, How or Why. Eric goes further, and allows you to answer the question: Who?
Eric's intelligence is dazzling; his knowledge of the human soul is astonishing..."

Fabian Delahaut, Business Coach
Author and Founder of Eagle Academy

"Drive, strategic thinking, empowerment. If you are looking for ways to multiply your business by ten, Eric Béhanzin will be able to ask you the very question that will make you think for three whole days (no less!), and transform your relationship with business."

Maryse Lehoux, Founder of Diva Yoga

MY GIFT TO YOU

Receive a free coaching session to make ten million in sales revenue.

We have decided to work with outstanding entrepreneurs.

However, there are some application requirements:

- At least one million euros in annual sales revenue,
- At least three regular employees (employed or self-employed),
- The motivation to make ten million in sales revenue within 18 months.

You will then be able to develop the three fundamental pillars that a business leader must implement to increase the company's revenue, namely:

1. **Clarity**: a clear vision and culture that everyone understands;
2. **Focus**: concentrate <u>only</u> on actions that can have a massive impact;
3. **Courage**: be ready to transform the company <u>radically</u> if necessary.

If you implement these three pillars, your growth will be exponential.

Here's what you need to do:

- Complete the form you will find at the link below: http://explosivebusiness.com;
- Confirm your registration;
- Complete the application questionnaire.

When you are selected, **you will receive a free coaching session** with one of our coaches/consultants to make ten million in sales revenue.

You deserve the best.

Yours, Eric.

VIDEOS

Here are the links to the videos that I filmed while I was writing the book. Access to the videos is free.

Day 1: http://12days.co/01

Day 2: http://12days.co/02

Day 3: http://12days.co/03

Day 4: http://12days.co/04

Day 5: http://12days.co/05

Day 6: http://12days.co/06

Day 7: http://12days.co/07

Day 8: http://12days.co/08

Day 9: http://12days.co/09

Day 10: http://12days.co/10

Day 11: http://12days.co/11

Day 12: http://12days.co/12

Day 13: http://12days.co/13

ACKNOWLEDGMENTS

I am forever grateful to the Creator for giving me every single one of these 12 days, the breath of life and the strength to finish this book that was a mountain for me to climb. **Life is wonderful with You.**

I would like to thank my parents. You found the patience to share everything that was really important to you. I hope you are as proud of me as I am happy to have you in my life. I think of my two little sisters and their mother, who, for all these years, have always shown their unconditional love despite my absence. **I love you all, dearly.**

Sabrina, you are a beacon of resilience, courage and generosity. **Thank you for giving so much of yourself** over the years, so that I could reveal the leader inside me.

Catherine, you are a living legend, your couple and your children serve as a model for me. **Please continue to inspire the people** around you.

Beka, my brother in arms in music, we have grown together, there is no denying that you are talented: persevere, because you deserve it.

Thanks to my singing and music mentors: Marcel Boungou, Régine and Denis Lapassion, Martin Guimbellot, you left your indelible imprint on me. You have my deepest gratitude.

Laurent, the passionate historian, I still remember our endless discussions about life. Your culture has always been an inspiration to me.

Guillaume, Norédine, I remember those darts games and your drinking nights... Babeth, those hours we spent on the phone putting the world to rights, Erwan B and Nolwenn, I came to know the Father at your own father's funeral, thank you for that.

Marie Claude and Erwan C, you were there for me, you gave me shelter when no one believed in me. I'm here for you now, whatever you need.

Gérard, my composition, harmony and counterpoint master. Christophe, my singing teacher, thank you for introducing me to music professionally.

Thank you, Myriam N, for your patience during those many months when you were certainly being challenged! But you have always persevered and it has paid off: I was lost and I now I'm found!

Thank you, my Patachou, you have been a safe refuge, you made so many sacrifices to offer me shelter for many months when I had nowhere to live. You have a *heart of flesh*, never let go of it.

I would also like to thank the whole team at CDC France who allowed me to take 12 days off work to write this book: Aurore, Betty, Carine, **you do an amazing job**. Without you, this book would have never seen the light of day.

I would also like to mention Jérôme, my relentless business coach who always pushes me to my limits; JT Foxx, my mentor, who allowed me to make a quantum leap into business and leadership; the coaches and members of the various mastermind groups I belong to; Maryse the diva, the dynamic Stéphanie, Martin, the super salesman, Annie, the funny coach, as well as Fabian, the marketing artist, Luc, Mr. No stress, Joel, the great golf coach, David, the word wizard, Leandro, the genius web marketer (you are the best!), Isabelle, the web embroiderer who moves mountains, Kevin, the super strategist, Yvan, my little brother, Jessie, the quiet force, Juliet, my writing coach, Coach Marco, who turned my brain upside down in just one day, and everyone I failed to mention simply because of lack of space here. **You are in my thoughts.**

Eric Célérier, thank you for being you! The months I have spent with you have allowed me to discover how **to be hyper-influential and benefit others, regardless of my imperfections**. You are an amazing leader!

Xav, Jean D, Pierre, Liliane, thank you for being there all these years, **you have extraordinary potential** which deserves to be revealed!

Claudiu, you contributed to freeing my potential as a History maker in this world. I could never forget you, Brother.

Finally, I would like to honor **Beehann**, an amazing woman and artist (GMO, private joke...) who supported me all these years, before finally becoming who she is today. **You deserve everything** you are, what you do and what you have. **Thank you for your patience and all your wise advice** that I did not always put into practice right away...

IMPORTANT NOTE

From the next page onwards, the book is divided into two parts.

The pages on the left present the simple 12-step method to become rich, happy and proud of yourself.
The pages on the right are given over to the writing experience for this first book, what I went through during my 12-day fast, without food or water.

There are three ways to read this book:

1. **The fastest:** simply read the boxes at the end of each chapter on the left-hand pages. This lays out the complete method, and it can be applied directly.
2. **The most logical:** read all the left-hand pages and you'll have the step-by-step rational technique for reaching these same conclusions. It's common sense, it is all laid out, and there is no trap!
3. **The most in-depth:** read the pages on the left, the pages on the right, and watch the daily videos, then you will understand what led me to experience this 12-day dry fast; why I set myself the challenge of finishing this book in such a short time, and you will also gain insight into my life's story and thoughts on some key issues that will gradually be revealed...

I hope you will choose the option that suits you best. Just keep in mind that if you only do the first two, you will certainly miss out on the essence of the book.

FOREWORD (Left-hand page)

Why "12 Days?" That's the time you need to earn a million euros if you earn one euro per second[1].

The purpose of this book is to give you the 12 simple and powerful steps that I have discovered in order to ensure that your business experience is meaningful, fruitful and enjoyable. I have chosen to write down these solutions so that you can be proud of yourself at the end of your life...

Proud to have taken care of those who are closest to you, proud to have accomplished the mission entrusted to you by the Creator of the Universe (nothing less), proud to have contributed in making a difference through the responsibilities you held.

After reading this book, you won't be able to say that you did not know. Ignorance is fatal. That's why I want you to know, and I want you to put everything into practice.

Here are three things to consider right now, on your way to becoming rich, happy and proud of yourself.

1. **Time is not linear.** You may be able to understand in **30 seconds** what someone else will understand in **30 years**. And vice versa. You can make extraordinary progress, mechanically, in a very short time. This discovery alone has transformed how I think.

---

[1] This is a financial reference to Anthony Robbins' book. For more information, see Chapter 7 (left-hand pages).

FOREWORD (Right-hand page)

Why "12 Days?" Because I decided to write this book in **12 days**, during a **dry fast**. I did not eat or drink because my aim was to achieve a complete physical, mental and spiritual rest. It was an extraordinary experience.

Do not try this yourself unless you have medical supervision.

Most people thought I was crazy. The most ignorant would tell me that one couldn't go for such a long time without food, and others would say that it is possible, but not without water.

Of course, this was not my first fast and I strongly advise against it if you are afraid or ignorant, because that is when disasters happen.

But after a lot of research and personal experiences, I came to the conclusion that **it is possible to go several weeks without eating AND drinking any water**.

So, I simply decided to spend the time alone, and experience it for myself. My assistant Betty rented a house for me in north of France for 12 days so that I could rest.

2. You always have a choice. Whatever happens to you, you have **free will**: the ability to decide what you want to be, do or have, according to these events.

3. Stop wondering how you can be rich, happy and proud of yourself, and start asking yourself why. You have no control over time, circumstances, or other people. If you stay focused on how, when things don't work out the way you want, you won't have the strength to bounce back and keep going. However, if you focus on your reason why, you will always find a way to get everything you really want, whatever obstacles may come up against you.

Now it's up to you to **use this book as a manual** that will allow you to recreate your life, following your own rules. I will take the time to explain what I mean in Chapter 1.

You will find a clear and orderly process that will help to bring out what is extraordinary in you. You will get to know yourself in depth. The first four chapters cover this. Then the next four chapters are about how to bring massive value to others and receive a lot of money in return. Finally, we will spend the last four chapters finding out how you can reach your happiness benchmarks and how that can help you contribute to the happiness of humanity as a whole.

I will be as direct as possible because **I want you to make it through the end of the book**. There will be quotes at the beginning and summaries at the end of each chapter, to recap the essential elements. So, there is **no need to read every word** to understand the main message.

The number 12 is the symbol of fullness, of completion.

My hope is that you spend 12 days reading this book and that you too can experience profound rest and restoration as I did when I was writing it.

Your time on Earth is limited, so make it count. Let me explain: every minute you spend asking deep questions about the meaning of your life, you will make tremendous progress and in just a few days, you will come to understand what many people only achieve in a few years.

The more you relax and increase your level of awareness, the less afraid you will feel, and the more you will dare to live by your own rules.

While the left-hand pages are very serious and practical, with a very specific objective, the right-hand pages are given over to the emotional and spiritual aspects of this experience.

Day after day, I'll tell you about my feelings, my thoughts, and my emotions, as well as the impact that the retreat is having on me.

The quest for truth is definitely the essence of this experience. Feeling that truth in my very being and publishing about it is new for me, because I usually present pragmatic and solid content.

I hope to humbly share my soul with you over the (right hand) pages of this book.

The benefit with this layout is that you can move from one page to another depending on the type of brain you have.

This book is far from perfect, both in substance and in form, but I have a feeling that it offers a solution to a deep-seated need. You are holding it right now, so my intuition must be right.

Commit to finishing, writing down and applying whatever you find relevant in this book to fulfill its promises, which are: **becoming a rich, happy and proud entrepreneur.**

You can seek guidance from a team dedicated to making you succeed at the link below:

http : //explosivebusiness.com.

The world needs you.

Happy reading.

If you are left-brained, which means you are mostly rational and logical, then you will be more interested in the pages that present the 12 keys to becoming rich, happy and proud of yourself.

If you are right-brained, more emotionally and creatively inclined, you will be more interested in the life experience that I will talk about, which involved 12 days of dry fasting: that is to say 12 days without eating or drinking.

Whatever you do, I hope you will draw some fundamental lessons from it and apply them throughout for your life.

You can seek guidance from a team dedicated to your success at the link below:

http://explosivebusiness.com

You deserve the best.

Happy reading.

Chapter 1: What Would You Do If You Had 30 Seconds Left to Live?

"The most civilized people are those who spread the most ideas, and those for whom ideas are worth more than goods."
Jean-Napoléon Vernier

I can't stand failure. Or the true nature of failure: **a person who gives up** on their dream because it's difficult.

So why do I hate to see someone give up? Because life is never linear, but exponential. I will talk about that in Chapter 8. Let's make it simple, you can struggle for years without seeing any real results then one day you have a breakthrough and your life changes overnight. And from then on, everything speeds up.

That's how I became a professional singer in 2002. I had been devoting myself to music for eight years. I hadn't decided to be a professional singer, but I played bass guitar for years. Then, in the space of a few weeks, I started working with some of the best French gospel artists and took part in international tours visiting more than a dozen countries.

What did I learn from that? **Perseverance pays off**.

I was able to identify this as one of my main values. I never give up. It's an integral part of me now, because my experience has allowed me to develop it.

Day 1: Dream[2]

12 days of dry fasting... What has brought me to do this?! Surely, people will think that I am crazy, dangerous, and suicidal.

It didn't matter to me, I had made my choice, I wouldn't go back. My loved ones were most afraid for me. So, I didn't give them all the details... That's right, I didn't advertise the part about dry fasting, if you know what I mean...

In fact, I am used to fasting, whether intermittently (one meal a day), which I do every day, or liquid fasting, that I managed to keep up for up to 11 and a half days almost 15 years before I wrote this book.

The longest dry fast (without water), that I have done twice so far, lasted four days and a half. I didn't stop for health reasons, but because my friends and family were worried.

I believe that fasting certainly possesses a spiritual dimension, but it also became about the physical and mental aspects, because research helped me to understand that it can be an opportunity to achieve extraordinary vitality and serenity.

My assistant booked a house for me, and explained that there were only a few places nearby where I could get necessities. I told her that it would be ok. The driver came to pick me up early in the afternoon, in a beautiful black sedan. He asked me if I wanted to listen to a particular radio station, I said I didn't, because I wanted to sleep during the trip.

---

[2] Watch the video for Day 1: http://12days.co/01

Why is it important to identify your true values?

Because your values define you. If someone ridicules one of your values, you will get very angry or extremely sad, and it can affect you more than if it had been for something else.

Remember that you didn't choose your birthplace, your parents, or some of the unfortunate circumstances you may have encountered during your life.

Therefore, you have your own personal story. Your life's milestones have given you moral qualities that drive you to act or react toward them: these are your personal values.

Differences in values are often a source of conflict.

Rules, laws or principles stem from these values, and they act as your life's rail tracks.

By making decisions based on your values and not on fleeting emotions, **you will achieve perfect stability**.

Have you identified any values that you hold on to, even if it means losing out on some things? These values might include freedom, truth, justice, family, compassion, integrity, etc.

Let's be practical: the following questions will help you identify at least three of your values.

To find out what they are, ask yourself these three sets of questions:

Just 48 hours ago, I didn't know that I would spend a portion of my days writing a book. I only realized what I would talk about when I arrived at the house, for the left-hand pages at least.

Because like many people, I prioritized the use of my left brain. Through the years, I have learned to listen to my intuitions and emotions when I make decisions, when I act, or when I have to realign myself, etc. The left-hand part of the book is very structured, whereas when I wrote the right-hand side, I just went with the flow.

The owner gives me a warm welcome, telling me he would stop by from time to time. He insists on taking me to the store, because the village has nothing. Apparently, everyone is concerned about my eating! I think long and hard, and then accept his offer, but I need a ploy to justify how little food I am going to buy.

When I get to the store, I have a stroke of genius: I choose dried fruit and nuts that will keep for the entire stay, and beyond. So, his mind is put to rest, and I have a choice, AND a backup plan.

If I can't manage it, I will have something to eat.

Then I go back to the house and start writing the book. An idea births in me: why not write a double book? Like in the book *The One Minute Millionaire*[3], the pages on the left are written for the left brain and the pages on the right are written for the right brain.

---

[3] By Mark V. Hansen and Robert G. Allen

1. What do your loved ones see as your best and worst character traits?

2. What circumstances in your life have caused you to feel intense anger? What gets you outraged?

3. What radical decisions have you made as a result of shocks, pain or revelations?

Based on your answers, identify your values and rank them in order of importance.

For example, my main values are freedom, perseverance and exceeding what you think you can do.

Then write the answer to this question: **"If you had 30 seconds to live, what instructions would you give to the person you love most in the world?"**

Take a break, find something to write with, and answer that question. Pick the book back up when you are done.

This answer is your personal message, not only to the world, but to yourself.

From now on, commit to respecting your values and reading your message every day to remind yourself of what truly matters.

You will find my personal message at the end of this book, just after Chapter 12.

My only worry is that I don't know what I'm going to write about for the right-hand side.

As I get more deeply involved in the writing process, it is becoming clear: I'll talk about what led me to write the book and, on the 12 days of dry fasting.

But before coming to why I wrote this book, **I am going to tell you my life story.**

0 to 7 Years Old: Dream
I was born in Paris to parents of color (which may not come as a surprise if you have seen my picture on the back cover). My mother is from Guadeloupe and my father from Benin and Togo.

They met in Paris and got married the year before I was born. I have very few memories of my childhood, except for some specific facts:

- I was born on June 6th (the day of the 1944 Normandy landings),
- I loved food,
- I started speaking at 4 (yes, I know, but the same is also true for Einstein!),
- I walked at 1 (on my actual birthday).

I started school happily. I was a good student, and my father, a former math teacher, ensured that I worked at home, so I learned to read and count early on.
When I was eight, we had to move and I skipped a year... I had a strict upbringing, hugs and kisses were few and far apart, but I understood a few decades later that displays of affection are not really part of Afro-Caribbean cultures.

Children obey, Period.

Well done, you've reached the end of the first chapter. Here's a summary:

---

1. Your values are moral qualities that derive from your own personal story.

2. They shape the rules you set for your life.

3. Identifying and ranking them helps you make the best decisions.

4. Answer these three questions to identify your three most important values:
—What do your loved ones see as your best and worst character traits?
—What circumstances in your life caused you to feel intense anger? What gets you outraged?
—What radical decisions have you made as a result of shocks, pain or revelations?

5. If you had 30 seconds to live, what instructions would you give to the person you love most in the world?
Write down the message and read it every day.

Something began to emerge in my character, a rebellious side that would put my father through his paces, especially during the second part of my life.

But for now, I am done with the first part.

I have also reached the end of the first dry fasting day. I don't have anything special to say because I am used to only eating one meal a day anyway. I feel some slight hunger pangs in the afternoon, but I know that my body has adapted, it is able to draw on its reserves.

I fall asleep serene and relaxed, not fully realizing the extent of the work that lies ahead.

Chapter 2: Your Mission, Should You Choose to Accept It

"The two most important days in your life are the day you are born and the day you find out why."
Mark Twain

You are unique. The combination of your talents, your passions and your past means that there is no one else like you in the world. Who would have thought that a previously shy boy like me who became a professional gospel singer would go on to become an author, speaker and business coach for entrepreneurs that make millions?

Let me tell you how I made it here.

It was in 2011. I was involved in many different associations as a teacher, and one of them asked me to join its committee, taking up a salaried position.
I was stunned because I wasn't expecting the offer. I was a professional singer and had already been running my own singing school for several years. It was working out pretty well. I was able to pay myself a salary and some of my colleagues were working there on a voluntary basis.

This opportunity shook me deeply. I began to imagine how I could juggle working with this association, running my school, and still manage everything else that was going on in my life. I struggled to decide.

I was already working a lot, I spent a lot of time commuting (at that time, I lived outside Paris) and I was finding it hard to make a living.

Day 2: Nightmare[4]

I wake up this morning at 8 am, but I laze in bed until 10:30 am. I'm supposed to be resting, aren't I?

I decide to shave my beard AND my head, which isn't an easy task, because I use a safety razor (as used in the army during World War II), a shaving brush, and soap.

It doesn't cause irritation and in the long run saves a lot of money, especially in terms of blades and soap. I take my time to prevent cutting myself as much as possible and I come out of the bathroom an hour and a half later.

I go up to the house's ground floor, which stands in a natural part of the forest, which stretches over several miles.

Just then, **I see a hare** on the premises. Wow! I'm amazed, I usually only see them on TV, in photos or on my dinner plate in the fall (I'm joking about the dinner plate, I actually eat very little meat, and only when someone else is cooking).

I start my second chapter which gives me a little more trouble, because it contains more data to include, cross check, and summarize.

I come to realize that writing a book is not that easy, even if you have all your data. I feel bad for novelists who have no choice but to find inspiration...

---

[4] Watch the video for Day 2: http://12days.co/02

Following some conflict that I won't go into here[5], the offer from the association was withdrawn. However, it did encourage me to ask myself a fundamental question:

What on earth am I here for? What legacy do I want to leave behind?

That's when I went on my first retreat away from home. I took a week, out of which three days were spent doing a water fast. Just then, I had several revelations, and one question struck me:

If you were not paid for this project, would you do it?

The answer was clear: **no**.

I then began to list everything I was doing, asking myself the same question, and I came to the same conclusion. I decided to stop almost everything. All I had left was the singing school that I managed. But it needed to take a new direction, better aligned with who I am, because I was exhausted and my students too.

So I started reading books by various authors like Stephen Covey, Jim Collins, and Tony Robbins. I understood that I had a mission to accomplish, and that understanding that mission would allow me to be better aligned with who I am, bringing much more value to others, allowing me to be more successful in every area of my life.

In 2013, I decided to invest hundreds of thousands of euros in strategy, marketing, sales, as well as in masterminds, coaching, and seminars, and I had to travel to several countries (the United States, Ukraine, Spain, United Kingdom, etc.).

---

[5] For the details, go to the right-hand pages on Day 5

Moreover, with my page layout idea with left-hand and right-hand pages, I have twice as much trouble and twice as much work, because I need to match the lengths of each "book" which is divided into twelve parts each...

12 keys on the left and 12 days on the right...

Well, in terms of energy I'm fine, I'm doing my morning ritual[6], so I'm well awake.

When I've finished and read several times back over the first two chapters, I decide to make a video each day to tell my story. While filming one of them, **I notice two owls** which come to settle just a few steps away from me. It's wonderful! I really didn't expect to see so many neighbors of this type.

The owner had told me about living in the country, but this really is something else. Am I really ready to face the forest? Yesterday, I went out to look around, but without a map, compass or smartphone, I quickly went back home.

I go for a walk in the village. It's hot, there isn't much noise, not much happens here. I walk toward the village church. I walk down the path, cross the cemetery, and go through the door. A gentle coolness sweeps over me, soothing me after the heat I have just been enduring outside.

It makes me think of the church in which I had my revelation, at my school friend's father's funeral. I was asked to sing "Amazing Grace" by John Newton. I will go into details on Day 4.

---

[6] I describe my morning ritual in Chapter 8, on the left-hand pages, tip 5

In the space of three years, I radically transformed my singing school, transitioned it online, and started offering business coaching.

I multiplied my cash flow by 20 and some of my offers by 100. After achieving these exceptional results, I launched the **Explosive Business** brand.

The flagship product is a program that enables entrepreneurs to **add ten million in sales revenue in a few months.** I'll talk about it in Chapter 7.

For more information about this program, visit: http://explosivebusiness.com.

My life's mission or **vocation** is then extremely clear, and I'm going to tell you about it in this chapter. I will also explain how I discovered it, and how you can achieve this same clarity.

Nobody can predict the future, but we can understand the present.

Our vocation is what determines our identity.

Here is a telling example: an object designed for people to sit on around a table is called a chair. If it is broken, and can no longer perform its function, it is just a useless piece of wood. Therefore, if you discover your vocation, you will know who you are, and what you really want (we will get into that in Chapter 3).

So I sing. "Amazing grace, how sweet th̲
like me! I once was lost, but now I'm found,

What could ring truer?

I leave the church and head out of the village. As
sign, I decide to record my second video.

On the way back, I take a detour. I go past the closed ⎯ and
find myself in front **a truck selling groceries**!

The country is full of surprises for an urban dweller like me! The van
is selling fruits, vegetables, cheese, cold cuts, and more. All the things
you can usually buy at a normal grocery store.

Wow! It is highly unusual for me here, and the quality of life is so
different: everyone says hello! That is unheard of in Paris...

When I get home, I realize that there is a second book I should write
in addition to the first. The one you are reading right now.

So I go back to writing until after midnight...

<u>**From 7 to 14 Years Old: Nightmare**</u>: My schooling is fairly
normal, except that my parents' relationship begins breaking apart. I
gradually lose my bearings.

...e combination of a three-part list:
- **...r passions;**
- **Your ultra-skills;**
- **Your personal story.**

By cross-referencing these three elements, you will find out what your vocation is. The difficulty lies in putting it all together to create a coherent and specific "whole." If you stick faithfully to this concept, you will never go off track.

Let's start with the first list: your passions.
Passion is the most powerful driver.

The word "passion" comes from the Greek term "pathos" which means pain. In other words, a passion is not something you just "like," it is actually like a fire burning inside of you. It is the kind of activity that fills you up and energizes you, something you can spend hours doing without realizing it. You feel better after doing it, and you don't even feel hunger when you are immersed in it.

In the light of this definition, write a list of your passions.

Here are some examples of passions: tennis, cooking, painting, video games, children between three and six years old, ballet, finance, board games, etc.

Here is a list of my passions:
—Leadership;
—Growth leverage;
—Strategy coaching;
—Inspiring others;
—Teaching.

I become more and more disobedient, I stop working, and refuse to do my father's additional homework. I lie, but I always get caught.

I am beaten more often. One day, my mother tells me not to go to school. At the time, I don't understand, but a few years later, I realize that if I had gone to school with a lump on my forehead, a swollen face and a fat lip, I would have perhaps been put into social services care, and could have been taken away from my parents.

At that time, I wonder about something: **"What is life for? Why is it so unfair?"**

Almost 25 years later, I have found the answer... **Life is for accomplishing a specific mission. It's not unfair, quite the opposite, it gives you a chance to turn evil into good**.

I start hanging out after school, but nothing serious, apart from wanting to run away from home and have a little fun. At the age of ten, a friend shows me some adult films and toys belonging to his parents. I feel upset, and find it disgusting, but I learn that this is how babies are made...

Relationships at home are getting worse, and we move to Paris. I join a prestigious high school that puts enormous pressure on its students. I grow up as good as I can, alone.

I meet students who shut me out. I'm not good enough to be at the top of the class, to be the one everyone turns to for answers, and I'm not popular at all.

No popularity = No girlfriend.

Then, the second list: your ultra-skills.

Ultra-skills enable you to bring extraordinary value to others.

I admit that that word doesn't exist at the time of writing, so feel free to replace it with *strengths, gifts* or *exceptional talents*. You are genetically programed for these things. They are natural to you, you find them easy, your brain and your hands work together with such speed that those around you don't understand how you do it.

Here are some examples of ultra-skills: organizing events, cake baking, writing articles, composing songs, interior decorating, managing money, creating a great atmosphere at parties, etc.

Here is a list of my ultra-skills:
—Simplifying complex ideas;
—Persuading others;
—Making connections between distant elements;
—Managing artists and staging;
—Turning good into excellent;
—Seeing far and big.

And finally, the last element: your personal story.
Your personal story makes you irrefutable.

List the highlights from your life. Think about your experiences, what has had a positive and a negative impact on you: traumas, victories, memorable encounters, transformations you have experienced, etc.

Around this time, I begin suffering from anxiety, thinking about death. **One day, I will no longer exist**.

I think about it every night, and it leaves me with chills. How is it possible to imagine that my existence will be lost in outer space?

OK, I don't use those exact words, but the fear is paralyzing. I start falling asleep increasingly late.

I gradually get used to the pace of life at school, but I start feeling increasingly angrier about school in general, and about my father who is utterly determined for me to have the best grades.

I end up living a life I hate, oscillating between a hypocritical school with no regard for its students, and a climate of constant conflict between my parents, and between my parents and me.

I can't see a way out...

Without realizing it, I develop an ability to create connections between very distant things to find solutions.

I am almost a teenager, and I go to Guadeloupe every summer. It is nice to visit aunts and uncles at first, but over the years I get fed up.

Beach, cycling, mosquitoes, beach, cycling, etc.

I'm growing up physically, mentally, and this inner anger is also growing.

Here are some examples: traveling around the world in 18 months, being sexually assaulted at the age of 4 by a parent, becoming a pop star as a teenager, being cured of a serious illness after 15 years, surviving a terrorist attack, being adopted in a foreign country, etc.

Whatever the events are, choose the ones that have deeply impacted you.

Here are some examples from my personal story:
—Formerly shy boy who became a professional gospel singer and later a public speaker;
—Cured of back pain, allergies and lost 20 pounds by eating living foods;
—Created several companies despite banking restrictions, with social assistance (RSA solidarity allowance, Restos du Cœur Charity);
—Became an author despite having very bad grades in School.

When I looked at the three lists as a whole, here is the conclusion I came to:

Today, **as a leadership coach, my vocation is to inspire you to fulfill your life's mission and change the world by sharing your values.**

You may be wondering what has happened to music in all this. Rest assured, I use it a lot in all my programs, workshops and seminars.

It's up to you to take action!

I have no passion, no escape route, nothing to channel my aggressiveness. **I don't love my family**. Not my parents, nor my extended family, they are all hypocrites, they fight incessantly, and I see it all...

Just then, something occurs to me: "**I'm not happy**."

At the age of 13, I get knocked down by a car, right in front of my house. The concierge in my building tells my parents he saw me flying right over the car. The only thing I remember is that when I started crossing the road, I was sure there was enough time to get to the other side. Then it hit me... I try to get up, but I can't.

My right leg hurts, I feel pain in my ribs ... the firemen arrive and take me to hospital. I am diagnosed with head trauma and a triple fracture in my right ankle.

I have surgery that same evening. I wake up the next day with my leg in a cast. I find out that the driver is only 19 years old. He comes to visit me with his mom one day. He is ashamed of himself, poor boy. I know it's my own fault, and I tell him so, but it doesn't change much. I go home after a week. My relationship with my parents is rekindled, I become dependent on them, they have to wash me morning and evening, take care of me.

Then I go back to school and become the class favorite for a little over two months. But still no girlfriend on the horizon... So here we are now in the third part of my life: adolescence... But I'm going to keep that for Day 3.

Physically speaking, this second day of fasting is going pretty well.

Write your vocation statement, taking into account the three lists of elements.

One fundamental rule: **No passion or ultra-skill should be neglected**.

Well done, you've reached the end of the second chapter. Here is a summary:

---

1. Your mission or vocation determines your identity.

2. If you go off track with your vocation, you are lost.

3. Your vocation is the coming together of three lists of elements:
  - **Your passions;**
  - **Your ultra-skills;**
  - **Your personal story.**

4. Cross reference these three lists and write your vocation sentence.

5. No passion or ultra-skill should be neglected.

My heart starts beating a lot faster and I can feel parts of my digestive system making sounds. I can't say that I'm hungry and I don't feel unwell, only that when I get up too quickly I get slightly dizzy.

I work until one in the morning to finish the right-hand pages and to make sure I'm on schedule for the two books in one.

I don't do anything halfway. I feel tired later in the evening, but I do everything I can to fill in day-2 pages before going to bed.

In spite of the effort, I realize that as I am writing these pages, I am freeing myself from emotions and memories which I had spoken to almost nobody before.

Writing has the gift of liberating the one who dares to put to paper his feelings, thoughts, and decisions.

I am grateful to have the opportunity to share my experience, so that you can understand that success is not only for the lucky ones, but also for the chosen ones.

Many are called, but few are chosen. The chosen ones are those who choose themselves, those who qualify themselves, who give themselves the resources, who pay the price, to be a player and not a spectator.

Franck Nicolas, an expert in leadership psychology, said: "On a football field, spectators pay to watch, and players are paid to play." There are thousands of spectators, but only 22 players on the field.

Who would you like to be?

Chapter 3: What Do You Really Want?

"Vision is the art of seeing things that are invisible."
Jonathan Swift

"There is no passion to be found playing small." This quote from Nelson Mandela is unsettling. When I ask people to **imagine what the next 40 years of their lives will be like**, they look astonished.

It would appear that not everyone can see far into the future. And yet, without a major purpose for your life, you won't get far.

So, I have created or found some questions to help you work out your own vision for the next 30 or 40 years.

Everything is possible in 10, 20 or 40 years. And in even less time if you are accompanied. Defining what you really want over the decades to come means that you have to project yourself, create your future, and know who you really are.

That's why I wrote the previous two chapters. Your vocation is generic, timeless, it's inside your gut. Your vision is in front of you, it is created through your vocation, it is how you are going to apply your vocation in the time and space that are attributed to you.

When you have defined it, knowing what decisions you should make will become extraordinarily easy.

Day 3: Rebellion[7]

I wake up at 6:20, but I actually get up at 9:00. My left foot is itching. I have a patch of weeping eczema that I have been trying to get rid of naturally for months.

Since I started practicing hygienism[8], a lot has happened in my life. I no longer have backaches like I used to have over 12 years ago, I have lost about twenty pounds, I have a lot more energy, I no longer suffer from allergies, and the list goes on.

But my eczema is persistent, and I want to stop using cortisone cream, because it does not deal with the root of the problem, it stifles the symptom. Cortisone also penetrates my body, and becomes a toxin that I will have to get rid of anyway.

Modern medicine is a snake biting its own tail.

The breakdown of families, government corruption, pressure from pharmaceutical, agro-food, and technological lobbies all generate a self-destructive lifestyle that fosters constant stress.

As soon as we have symptoms, we race to the doctor for a prescription instead of just resting and letting the self-healing ability of the body do its work.

Natural medicine is no better, because it often starts from the same assumption: it is normal to be ill.

---

[7] Watch the video for Day 3: http://12days.co/03

[8] The approach to health that states that if you remove the cause, the disease will disappear.

Ask yourself, does this opportunity help me to achieve my vision? If so: DO IT! If not: refuse it.

"May your yes be yes, and your no be no, the rest comes from the devil..." There is nothing worse than doubt. It hurts more than anything else.

Now that you understand the importance of defining your vision, let's put it into practice.

A vision is clearly qualified and quantified:

Specific (clear, concrete, precise)
Measurable (have I succeeded or not?)
Attractive (I like the objective)
Realizable (it only depends on me)
Temporal (it has a time limit)

Here is a poor example of vision:
I want to succeed in business to inspire and help other people. What rubbish! It's far too vague, and it would be impossible to make a decision based on that!

Here is a good example of vision: *I want to open a chain of 1,000 Caribbean fast food restaurants specializing in chicken salads within 30 years based in France's major cities, starting with Paris. I'll create original recipes that are light, yet tasty, and I won't go over 400 calories for each product. My flagship product will be the "Smoked chicken with Espelette pepper" salad. I'll only use fresh ingredients, I'll only offer takeaway and I'll patent recyclable packaging so that my clients can eat the product easily while on the move.*

What if we simply focused on keeping an excellent health? Instead of finding a solution to cure a disease, why don't we seek to find out what really causes it?

By avoiding what causes our illnesses, the body can recover its optimal state. I'll talk about that in another chapter.

To get back to my fasting experience, Day 3 is very strange... After my morning ritual (which includes intensive exercise), I feel like my physical performance has skyrocketed, and that I have fewer breathing problems. My voice is very powerful and confident, it doesn't strain. When I sing in the shower, it's the same thing, my voice becomes extremely powerful and flexible, I sing very easily and with virtually no effort.

I don't feel weak at all, quite the contrary. I have this very strange feeling that I had already experienced more than 12 years ago, when I fasted for more than 11 and a half days!

I do not need to eat to live.

Am I becoming a crazy extremist? No, this feeling is clear and it isn't going away. I intend to observe myself over the next few days. I no longer feel like I am fasting, but rather controlling the elements within my body. My levels of consciousness and authority are increasing dramatically.

My intuition is that my weight will stabilize, and that I will not lose any more. Which is great for reassuring my friends and family.

Is this thinking just a fad?
Suddenly I feel very tired, so I go to sleep for most of the afternoon and then I will shoot my video.

With this profound idea: it is possible to eat healthy and enjoy it.

After 10 years, I will be offering face-to-face workshops and video training for people to cook healthily in order to stop obesity, diabetes, cardiovascular disease, arthritis and any other type of illness related to a poor diet.

This example of vision is much more precise. If this person was offered a partnership to open an Italian restaurant, they would refuse respectfully, because it is not part of their vision.

Choose some music you can relax to, sit in a quiet place, take notes and do these two exercises.

First exercise:

Imagine your life over the next 40 years. If your great-grandchildren were reading your life story, what would you like them to read about you? Include a lot of details, dates, locations, numbers, and highlights.

Second exercise:

Imagine your ideal day if you had all the money in the world, as well as unlimited resources and knowledge:

What time do you wake up? Where do you live? In which country? In what kind of house? Do you have children? Grandchildren? How much money do you make? What is your fitness level? Do you exercise? How long do you spend working? What are your hobbies?

From 14 to 21 Years Old: Rebellion

Adolescence has finally arrived. When I start high school, disaster strikes...
My schooling takes a nose dive. Even though I had skipped a year, I had to repeat my sophomore and junior years (science major). Perfect, since I hate school.

Once, when things get really bad with my familly, I'm so tired of being beaten in the mornings if I don't get up that one night I decide to sleep with a sharp knife. **"If he touches me, I kill him."**

Strangely, it never happened again. That morning, my father didn't say anything to me, nor did he say anything the following weeks. If I had killed him with that knife, where would I be today?

Life is a gift.

At the age of 16, following another clash with my father, I run away for the first time. My mother comes to pick me up. Then I escape again a few days later.

This time, I go with my mother to the police station to report my father for abuse. From that point on, there is no more physical violence. But I'm told that I need to get my bachelor's degree if I want to stay living at home.

At the age of 18, I expect to be sent away from home, but nothing happens. I buy my first guitar and I immerse myself in my passion for music. Finally, the last year of high school begins. The teachers are no longer the ones who will decide if I can move to the next level, it's up to me now. **When I pass my exams, I'll be free**.

These exercises aren't easy, but they'll help you over the coming years. You should do them several times a year to make sure they're still true and relevant.

Write with no restraint.
When you create your own future, you become the master of your life.

And now, we've come to the end of the third chapter, so here is the summary of the essential concepts:

---

1. Everything is possible in 10, 20 or 40 years.

2. A vision is clearly qualified and quantified:
Specific (clear, concrete, precise)
Measurable (have I succeeded or not)
Attractive (I like the objective)
Realizable (it only depends on me)
Temporal (it has a time limit)

3. A vision lets you know what decision to make.

4. Imagine your life over the next 40 years. If your great-grandchildren were reading your biography, what would you like them to read about?

5. Imagine your ideal day, if you had all the money in the world, as well as unlimited resources and knowledge.

6. When you create your own future, you become the master of your life.

During my senior year at school, my father and I do not speak at all. After I am given a disastrous grade when I take the mock exam in February, I realize that I won't pass if I go on like this. I decide to team up with a friend to work hard to succeed. In the end, **I pass my bachelor's degree on the first try**!

My parents pay holidays to Benin for me to see my father's family whom I met three years earlier when I visited the country for the first time. Through my cousins, I find out that the adults want me to stay and **study in Africa. What a nightmare!** I kick off, I make their life so awful that they take me straight to the airport.
When I get back to Paris, I find out that my belongings are in the cellar and that I'm not allowed to live at home. **My father no longer wants me in his house. My mother** can no longer put up with him, and **leaves**.

I stay with my childhood friend's parents while my mother goes to a women's shelter. My friend has gone to study in Belgium, so I take his place. Never in my life have I been treated with so much consideration, love and kindness. I gradually become a member of the family.
Then my mother gets an apartment, so I move in with her and start university. But I am still angry. I quit college after two years, without a degree. I am called up to serve in the army, which is compulsory at the time.

On the verge of suicide, I find out that I am to do my military service in Paris. So, I am there during the day and work in a fast food restaurant on evenings and weekends. I have to do this to pay my rent, because I am now sharing a flat. My roommate is a musician like me and then, inspired by him, **I decide to become a professional musician**...

That's the end of the third part of my life...

Chapter 4: Reveal your ultimate gift

"Understand that talent, without genius, means very little.
Doing easily what others find difficult is talent;
doing what is impossible is genius."
Gilbert Sinoué

Doing the impossible. Only your ultimate gift or your genius can help you achieve that. Steve Jobs said: "Everything around you that you call life was made up by people that were no smarter than you, once you learn that, you'll never be the same again."

Your ultimate gift is inside you, here and now.

But you may not be aware of it. You may not have found it. Yet it is there, this unique ability that you have and that can allow you to achieve the impossible.

My goal in this chapter is to help you discover it. It will allow you to fulfill the gigantic vision that you defined in the previous chapter.

Without this ultimate gift, nothing is possible. With this ultimate gift, the world is in your hands. **Your ultimate gift is the unconscious response you have developed to the deepest pain you have experienced in your life**. It came about because of a "why." The greatest "why" of your life.

When you have found the point of greatest pain in your life, you will discover your "why." Your ultimate gift is the intrinsic response that you have developed as a result of this "why," this deep pain.

Day 4: Revelation[9]

*"Man has everything he needs to make
his own decisions. But the highest revelation.
is that God is in every man."*
Ralph Waldo Emerson

God is in every man. Thank you, Ralph, that's some meaningful stuff. Few people are aware of it, and yet it is the simple and ultimate truth.

This time I wanted to use a quote to support my point. It's my fourth day without eating or drinking. I feel a little feverish, so I sleep a lot and when I am not sleeping, I'm lying down. Except in the morning, when the owner of the house stops by, I stay in bed until 3:30 pm. Yes, I know ... but I'm here to rest, right?

And this book is a lot of work... Chapter 4 on the ultimate gift is exciting, it makes me grateful.

When I do my morning ritual, I realize that the exercise doesn't tire me. Quite the opposite, it gives me energy. **Movement is life**.

If you feel weak or tired, do some exercise. It works! I spent four days not eating, and after a one-minute run in place, I feel much better. Then I take a shower, a cold one. I've been doing that for a few days, to wake my body up, invigorate myself, and shorten the time I spend in the shower.

---

[9] Watch the video for Day 4: http://12days.co/04

So, it is essential to discover it, because it is the only tool you have to make this vision a reality, the impossible dream that you wrote about in the previous chapter.

One of my mentors has the ability to read people. In just a few seconds, he's able to say exactly why your business isn't successful.

When coaching individual entrepreneurs, he used to charge one million euros for one day of coaching. His clients said it was worth it!

What is your ultimate gift? What makes you this unique and exceptional person, and will allow you to become financially rich?

Let's be clear: your finances are a reflection of the monumental value you bring to others. For example, if you sell a basic loaf of bread, your value is low. But if you sell the very best bread, to the point where the most influential presidents and kings crave it, then your value is enormous.

What makes you extraordinary? What do you do better than anyone else? Or like nobody else? Whatever this gift might be, look for it very carefully.

When you find it, you instantly become a god.

I know, this promise sounds exaggerated, yet you'd be amazed at just how much my clients pay me to help them solve their problems using my gift.

How can you discover your ultimate gift?

It's difficult, like it is every time, except that now my body seems to be craving it. These cold showers do me the world of good. Usually, I keep them short, but today I'm really enjoying the sensation.

I go back to writing the book. Two feelings are battling with each other: "It's hard and tedious, plus, it's two books in one, what a mad idea!" And another "Wow! What an amazing adventure, just imagine the millions of people who are going to read these pages!"

In the end, I finish Chapter 4 quite quickly. And then I wonder what I'm going to write about on the opposite pages. But in fact, as soon as I start talking about the fourth part of my life, my revelation, it will be pretty intense. So, let's get on with it.

From 21 to 28 Years Old: The Revelation

I have just decided to be a professional musician, I don't know what the future holds, but I spend time working hard on it. I have been practicing my new instrument for some time: the bass guitar. I take classes, and I am coached by my roommate who is three years younger than me, but who is extremely gifted musically. So, I practice bass for eight hours daily.

This is all during my free time after the army, of course. I am able to get my drivers' license for free with the army. Just another gift out of "nowhere" that I took for granted at the time.

By the way, my first girlfriends finally come into my life during the third part, I forgot to mention them. Things are hectic, I have no stable relationships, and I am certainly no poster boy for true romance.

To find out what it is, you need to look for something very subtle, a creative mechanism, a connection, a resolution that is always the same, that is inherent during the times in your life where you have shown yourself to be extraordinary.

For example, I coached singers for years, so how is it possible that I now coach entrepreneurs?

Do these two roles have anything in common? Yes, but it's not easy to make the connection at first.
Both involve passing a message to an audience.
Both desire to be liked by that audience.

I know it's not very convincing. However, I've come to realize that there wasn't a huge difference between **Steve Jobs and Michael Jackson**. Both were **rock stars**.

Whenever they made an appearance, people hurried to get a glimpse of them. At whatever the cost, place or time. If their name appeared on a poster, everyone would flock to the event!

I have the gift of turning people into rock stars, I find what is exceptional about them, I make them aware of it, and they become extremely confident, and perform outstandingly well in front of an audience.

When I really examined my character, I noticed that I spend my time looking for the one detail that makes a huge difference in a person. When I find it, I highlight it, until my clients are aware of it too. It becomes obvious. And all of a sudden, their world is transformed.

They can use their ultimate gift as much as they like, for the rest of their lives.

I end up having many odd jobs, I don't want anything that take up too much time, because my goal is set on music... In order to focus on work, I refuse to join a music group for years.

I start working at a telemarketing company that is quite famous at the time, and pays very well. I like telemarketing: it's a lot less tiring than fast food, and it pays better if you're good at it. Because your pay is based on performance, not time spent. No results = no money. This time in my life is quite a challenge.

I meet a singer who has signed with a big record label, and we decide to work together. She tells me all about her experience of show business. The project lasts for several months, we compose some music, and I am introduced to the manager, and to the record label. I think: "Finally, all my efforts are going to pay off!" One day, I find out that I have been taken off the project. Boom! I take a real blow. *Go home, kid... There's nothing for you here, goodbye...*
I pick myself back up and start creating new projects, I met artists, I record other songs, then with an old friend of mine, I decide to take part in a gospel workshop.

I think: "Wow! Gospel is serious stuff, it's about God and the singers have beautiful voices!" I sign up for it and instantly fall in love. I love coming to sing every week, and at the end of the year the choir director asks me if I would like to join his semi-professional choir the following year! What an honor!

So, I come to the first rehearsal. Everyone is chatting and laughing, and then at one point, just before starting, everyone stops to pray.

My clients are completely transformed. And that's what I want for you now. As Steve Jobs said, apply what I'm telling you, and "your life will never be the same again."

Are you ready?

Let's do it!

1. Think about all the times in your life where you have proven to be exceptional, whether in your career or your personal life. Don't look for any links between them just yet. Think about all the times when you thought all was lost or good results seemed unlikely to happen, but you did achieve the impossible. Make a list of them now. Then come back to reading this book.

2. Well done, you've completed the first step. Now, ask yourself why it was so important to achieve the end result. What caused this outcome? Why were you so involved? What do all these "why" have in common?

3. Have you found the "why" for each event? Great! Now, look for the operating method, the subtle intellectual process that you put into practice to achieve the impossible. What do all these successes have in common?

When you have these three answers, focus on your big "why" and find the unconscious response that you have developed (without realizing it), and used to solve it.

Here is my example to help you.
My "why": my father wanted me to have excellent grades in school. So, he would leave me at my desk for hours trying to solve math problems that he took from his own school books.

I lower my head as a sign of respect and I listen. Then the rehearsal begins.

I watch the musicians and singers attentively, and I realize that I can do what they do, if I am prepared to work. I take singing lessons with a teacher who was trained in the United States, and he gives me a solid foundation for two and a half years. I am making progress at high speed because I still have my goal in mind: **becoming a professional artist.**

I become a key member of the choir, I perform in concerts. The other singers, who were skeptical at first, are amazed by how much I am improving. We do some concerts in Paris, and my name begins to be known. I am offered other professional projects within the community, and I do more and more concerts. **My dream finally comes true!**

But one event really shakes my upcoming career. A childhood friend has just lost his father. I ask him if he would like me to sing at the funeral, and he agrees. It is one of my life's most memorable experiences.

On the morning of the funeral, I decide to sing Amazing Grace by John Newton. As I have only been singing Gospel for a short time, I learn the second verse on that same day. There are very few words in the song, but I am struggling to remember them all. I try and try, but I just can't get them into my head.

I have to leave, and on the way to the funeral, I still felt unsure about the lyrics to the second verse. So, for the first time in my life, I pray to this God, whom I don't know. The prayer is very short: "If you really exist, help me remember the lyrics. Not so that people

My inability to get results needed for my father to be proud of me was the most severe pain I felt in life. I was convinced, though it wasn't the case, that my father didn't love me.

My ultimate gift is my ability to find a tiny detail that will allow a person to achieve extraordinary result with very little work. I kept on creating links to find that detail. And that was the unconscious response I developed as a result of my experiences. **Behind all pain, there is a gift**.

I became lazy intelligent. I apply the principle of Pareto[10] 80/20, but to the extreme, that is to say 99/1.

1% of actions give 99% of results.

I used this gift to help entrepreneurs make millions in revenue. Of course, I also did training courses (I invested more than $130,000) in strategy, business, marketing, sales, finance, and systems to contribute this massive value.

Ultimate Gift + Massive Training = Massive Value

You will receive a lot of money in exchange for your massive value. So, be very diligent here!

You have the formula and the process to find everything for yourself, so now it's up to you!

Reveal your ultimate gift!

---

[10] Pareto principle : 20 % of our actions produce 80 % of our results.

will say that I sing well, but for my friend's family, so that it will be a positive experience for them."

I arrive at the chapel, the priest calls me forward, I get up and walk slowly towards the lectern. I can see them all, my friend, his mother, his sister, and his girlfriend two rows behind... The atmosphere is heavy, I close my eyes. But I hesitate. I think I hear a voice saying: "Do it now." So I begin...

I open my mouth without even thinking about my usual singing technique, but one thing strikes me. My voice doesn't sound like it usually does. I have a feeling that angels sing with me, my voice fills the chapel, yet, I don't feel like I am singing loudly...

I go to the notorious second verse, I feel feverish, and once again, I hear a voice saying, "Go on." I open my mouth, and out comes a smooth stream of lyrics, line after line. As soon as I finish one, I can't remember the one that should come next, but when I open my mouth, the words come out.

Throughout this entire time, I can feel a sort of quivering all over my body and something like a presence above me and to my left, but I don't know what it is. My eyes are closed. I finish the second verse, then I repeat the first verse more quietly, and then I stop.
When I open my eyes, my hands are outstretched, and I am crying. And just above me to my left, I can see a huge statue of Jesus on the cross...

I go back to my seat, dazed, and I can't remember the rest of the ceremony. In the end, when the priest asks believers to make one sign, and non-believers to make another, I know that I have to take a stand: **I make the sign of a believer**.

Here are the key concepts from Chapter 4 about your ultimate gift.

1. Your ultimate gift is inside you, here and now, and it is the heart of your vocation. It will help you to make your vision come true.

2. Your ultimate gift is the unconscious response to the deepest pain you have experienced in your life.

3. Your ultimate gift makes you extraordinary and turns you instantly into a rock star when you discover what it is. You will be able to use it as much as you want, for as long as you want.

4. Here are three exercises to find out what it is:
- Think about all the times in your life when you have proven to be exceptional, whether in your career or your personal life.
- Now, ask yourself why it was so important to achieve the end result. What do all these "why" have in common?
- Now, look for the operating method, the subtle intellectual process that you put into practice to achieve the impossible.

5. When you have these three answers, **focus on your big why and find the unconscious response that you have developed** (without realizing it), and that you used to solve it.

6. Ultimate Gift + Massive Training = Massive Value

At 26, I have just experienced the biggest revelation of my life:

God exists and I didn't know it.

If I have been wrong about that, then **everything I believed up to that point is potentially wrong!**

I realize that God has seen all my silliness, my thoughts, my wounds... But I feel no fear, only love, as though from a gigantic, transparent man who always had me in his sights. I feel naked in front of Him, but He is holding out his hand like a father, but this time it is a Heavenly Father.

If God exists, what does He want from me? What do I have to do? I decide to accept a book that a friend has given to me as a gift, because I am looking for the truth. The people I met sing Gospel music, just like I do professionally, so I am sure this is no coincidence.

I no longer believe things happen by chance.

So, I open the book from which the Gospel is taken...

And that's the end of the fourth part of my life...

I finish writing this part of the book at 1:00 in the morning. I am proud of myself because it wasn't easy. But now it's done.

I had filmed the daily video just before writing it to give me courage and it worked. It's always good to remember why we do things when we start getting discouraged.

Thank you.

Chapter 5: How Can You Attract Hoards of Clients?

"Whoever wishes to become great among you shall be your servant."

The Bible

It's time to start giving. But not just to anyone, nor anyhow. In the previous chapters, we have learned about the exceptional value you can bring to others, especially with your ultimate gift.

This massive value must be a value that is perceived by your audience. For this to happen, you must know your clients. Know what motivates them, what terrorizes them, what prevents them from sleeping at night. **What do they want more than anything and that they do not have yet?**

If you don't have an accurate understanding of your ideal client, there is no chance they will understand what you are offering. You must know where to find them. And this raises an important point.

I believe **the most effective way to become rich is to be an entrepreneur**. Not an employee, with someone setting out your monthly salary on your behalf. Entrepreneurs don't think in terms of monthly salary, but in annual revenue. Sometimes it rises, sometimes it falls, but there is an annual target.

What is your annual target for the end of your tax year, or for the next 12 months if the year is starting right now?

Once you have defined that target, you are ready to make money. The fastest way to make money is to create an offer, an exchange of value for money, which means **SELLING.**

Day 5: Religion[11]

Looking out of the window this morning, **I see a squirrel**. It's amazing, the ability these little animals have to climb trees, then to dart back down the other way without a care in the world.

The weather today is shifting between sunny spells and showers. So, it feels a little cooler, which I don't mind. I get up quite late (12:30 pm) although I woke up early (8:20 am). I like staying in bed without having to explain why.

I take another cold shower, and I get the same feeling I had the day before, especially as I allow the water to flow over the back of my neck. It feels wonderful, even though my muscles are tense.

I've definitely lost some weight. I am very thin, and I'm still urinating (sorry about the explicit details), even though I'm not drinking anything, which confirms the endogenous water theory. Water in gel form is released by the body as fat deposits are broken down, in order to nourish the body from the inside.

I realize that I haven't mentioned something that is actually very important. When you deprive yourself of food for a long time, the body is still fed: it seeks out its reserves. First come complex sugars, then, after three days, fats.

I don't feel nauseous, nor do I have a headache, because I am dry fasting. With water, this type of symptom is more frequent.

---

[11] Watch the video for Day 5: http://12days.co/05

If you are looking to sell easily and quickly, **you must create a Star Offer** that fulfills these three conditions:
- It must be irresistible to your client.
- It must be ultra profitable for you.
- It must be easy to deliver.

If it is irresistible to your client, it will be easy to sell. And you don't decide that, the market does. Not your sales pitches, nor your super bonuses, or mega-guarantees. The market decides. That means your clients. If they race to buy it, that means it's irresistible. If it isn't, you need to change your offer. It couldn't be simpler.

To create an irresistible offer, you need to:

- Have a clear and simple message. Do away with expert language, it will lose you a lot of money. If your clients can't understand you, they won't buy what you are offering.
- Offer your clients ten times the value of the cost of your offer, and your clients will think they are getting the deal of the century (and you should feel like you have been cheated).
- Have a product that is easy to consume, and not complicated, otherwise it will put your clients off.

Here is an example of a Star Offer I created for my first business venture, the online singing school:

- A short video course entitled "**Sing in tune in just 7 days**";
- The client receives an email with **a 10-minute video every day** for 7 days;
- It has a value of <u>$285 with the free bonuses,</u> but I made it available for **$67**;
- I offer a **money-back guarantee lasting 365 days.**

64

When I do my morning ritual, I still have the impression that my performance is increasing, I have greater flexibility, and I feel much lighter.

I procrastinate writing Chapter 5, although, I have already written one third of the book! I should be happy, just a week ago I didn't even know I would be in the process of writing my first book...

The owner ends up coming over to get some of his stuff, and I talk to him about the project. As soon as he leaves, I get started on it, and finish Chapter 5.

Let's continue with our story...

From 28 to 35 Years Old: Religion

I have made the most important discovery of my life, I want to shout it from the rooftops, but before, I have to put one or two things right. **I decide to forgive my father for everything**.

I go to see him two weeks after this event happened, and I give him the book I mentioned which talks about Gospel. I find out that I have a second younger sister, the family is growing (ah yes, I forgot to say in the previous section that my father had remarried).

We make amends, I start visiting him a little more often (it used to be just once a year for Christmas), and a new father-son relationship is born. And this time there is no more fear, and no more anger, only respect. I realize that I am just like him in many ways, much more than I thought.

My own spiritual quest takes on a new dimension. I begin looking for people who are living the same spirituality as I am, that thirst for knowing the God I have just encountered.

Everything comes together, it is ultra-profitable for me, because it is filmed and readily available, so, I have no effort to make. However many clients I have, I still make money, it is easy to deliver, because the whole process is automated online.

My rock star coaching offer for entrepreneurs takes a similar format. My promise is to **add ten million in sales revenue in a few months**. Even though the price tag may seem high for some entrepreneurs, it is just spare change when they go on to become multimillionaires.

I have a margin of 80% on this offer, which allows me to deliver comfortably, and it's easy because I choose the specific location, and the conditions. So, I have the edge.

For more information about this program, visit the website below: http://explosivebusiness.com.

IMPORTANT: **always calculate your margin** before setting your prices. Margin = Prices excluding taxes - Cost price

Cost = Deliverer's salary + Director's salary + Variable expenses + Fixed costs

Your first Star Offer must be enough to keep your company afloat. All your Stars Offers must be win-win deals.

What is your Star Offer? Are you sure that your clients understand your business? What massive value can you offer them? Can you describe it in simple terms and in one sentence? Are they struck by what it is saying? Is it easy for you to deliver? Automated or delegated?

I end up at a church where I take my first steps as a believer. I get baptized (at 29 years old), and in the same year, I perform at a concert for the *Fête de la Musique* Festival. After this concert, I become very well known in the community because hundreds of people have seen me performing on stage. I don't care about that just then, but it enhances my reputation, and makes it easier for me to join the community.

That same year, I founded my singing school, and by some miracle, I found myself with 72 students during the first year, even though people didn't really know me as a singing teacher! So, a new adventure begins. But I'm not alone.

I forgot to mention that I met Beehann in the first choir I joined. I no longer sing with that choir. She now works with me, and for all the years that follow, I am still teaching her to be a pianist, singer and choir director. She sings with an American voice and French sensitivity. Unbelievable...

Over the years that follow, I get involved not only in my own church, but in many others for which I begin taking on the role of musical director. I travel throughout the Paris region teaching music, or the Bible, or both at the same time. My new and alternative way of seeing things brings a refreshing change, and I am having a greater and greater impact, but I don't realize it at the time...

Until one day, when I receive an offer that came completely out of the blue... Really, completely... One of the pastors at another church invites to me to join their team as a **musical pastor**.

Wow! Who would have thought? Me, as a man of the Church?

If your main current offer does not sell fast and well, it's not a Star Offer. If you only make a little money on it, it's not a Star Offer. If it is difficult to deliver or requires too much investment, it's not a Star Offer.

IMPORTANT: Sell <u>BEFORE</u> you create your product.

This will allow you to test the market before creating a product that may not be wanted...

You need to act. Create your Star Offer if you do not have one yet, otherwise you could upgrade your main offer to a Star Offer.

Time for the summary now!

---

1. The fastest way to earn money is to SELL by becoming an entrepreneur.

2. What does your ideal client want more than anything, and that they do not have yet?

3. In order to sell easily and quickly, create a Star Offer. It fulfills three conditions:
- It's irresistible to your clients.
- It is ultra profitable for you.
- It is easy for you to deliver.

4. <u>Always calculate your margin</u> before setting your prices.

5. Sell <u>BEFORE</u> you create your product.

It is the first time I had to make such an important decision that would have an effect on the rest of my life.

I ask my pastors for advice, and at that point I am caught between a rock and a hard place. They don't agree, or rather they said: "If you want to leave, go!"

I am stunned... Nobody really knows what advice to give me. I think it may be beneficial for me as a leader, it is related to music, people do like me, but...

Something is bothering me...

The pastors of each church meet, argue, and make a decision... The offer is eventually withdrawn, but I am drained by the experience.

I decide to go on my first retreat back to nature to think about my life, because it is the first time that I ask myself this question:

What is my purpose on Earth? If the professional men of God don't have the answer, it means that it must be between Him and me.

That's when I finally understand who I am... And here ends the fifth part of my life...

And I'm thrilled to have gotten here this early, at 8:30 pm!

Chapter 6: How Do You Get What You Want From Other People?

"Persuasion is often more effective than force."
Aesop

People love buying, but they hate being sold to. SELLING is persuading your client that the best way for them to change their life or business is for them to buy your product. But the client must never be forced.

In this chapter, you will learn all about the **basics of elegant one-to-one selling.** The kind of selling where your client has decided to make a purchase, and they are eager to buy your product. The one where you don't sound like a used car salesperson. The one where you don't need to reel off a list of selling points: the client convinces themselves that the only solution available to them is to buy what you are offering.

So, here's what you need to make sure of before you begin:
1. You have a Star Offer, one that is based on their needs according to **the client's own words.**
2. Your product (though not perfect) is of very good quality, it meets their needs, and is endorsed by your ultimate gift.
3. You treat your client as though they were your best friend.

If these criteria are all met, then you will be able to use the simple tools that I am going to give you.

IMPORTANT: The difference between persuading and manipulating is your intention. When you persuade, you are aiming for a win-win, when you manipulate, it's a win-lose.

Day 6: Release [12]

I get up late because I had trouble sleeping the night before. I beat my previous "record" which was four days and a half of fasting. And last night has been plagued with anguish, fears of sudden death. So early in the morning, I get up to close the window...

Sometimes the solution can be very simple, all you need to do is close the window. Suddenly, I can no longer hear the sounds of nature and am able to get back to sleep very quickly.

I start writing Chapter 6, which this time is very dense, then I go back to bed. I get up again at 7 pm when my landlord comes to have a tractor delivered so that he can mow his lawn.

Just then, **I notice a deer** darting around the field. The grass has grown tall, but I can still see it. And it's quite a surprise for a city dweller like myself, I usually only see pigeons.

I take a nice cold shower, which does me a world of good, even though all my muscles are tense. This period of fasting is perhaps increasing my body temperature, like a minor fever. But I'm fine. I have a pasty mouth still, and need to rinse it three to four times a day. I'm still losing weight, but I feel confident. It'll stabilize at some point.

The days drag on for so long when you're not eating... There are no meals to prepare, season, cook, you don't need to set the table, do the dishes, wipe up...

---

[12] Watch the video for day 6: http://12days.co/06

Let's take a look at what selling is not:
- A series of selling points based on the features of your product;
- A detailed description of the benefits of your product over the competition;
- A long story about your company, its fame, certifications, etc.

That's narcissistic selling: me, me, and me. It doesn't work, or seldom works, and it's based on your own ego. So, forget that.

The client wants the conversation to be about them. So, let's see what selling can be:
- **Questions** based on their pain, their fears, what might happen if they don't take action right now;
- **Questions** based on their aspirations, their inspiring goals, and what might happen if they get the results they want;
- **Solutions** based on all their answers to both of these previous points that your product can provide.

Your product must be a stepping stone to making the client's dream come true. So, make it as simple, easy, and effective as possible, but don't describe it. Start with what the client really wants, and tell them how your product will help them get it.

If your product does not meet your client's expectations, don't sell it to them. Either you don't have the right client in front of you, or you don't have the right product, or you don't really know what your ideal client wants.

If either of these do not apply, don't sell them anything. Seriously. If you do, you'll have trouble with that client further down the line. I learned my lesson the hard way a few years ago.

I think I'm saving at least five hours a day... So when I am not writing I don't have much in the way of entertainment. The next time I decide to go on a retreat, I'll remember to bring something to read, or something fun to do.

So, I go on the Internet. I know it's not ideal for a retreat, but I've been looking for a good-quality camera with a microphone port for a long time to take 4K videos, and I've now found what I want! It relaxes me a bit before I get back to work.

I need to pay for the camera, so, I have to sell one of my business manager programs, but it should be fine, I'm waiting for answers from a few clients who seem very interested.

I have to say that I'd love to drink a large glass of cool water and one of refreshing vegetable juice right about now. I just need to wait for a few more days, and I can have all of that again. I sense that my dry fast is related to the writing of this book. It won't have the same impact if I don't write it under these conditions. It's just a feeling I have.
OK, I know, you're waiting for the rest of my story... Well, here it goes!

From the Ages of 35 to 42: Release

Following a period of confusion that was triggered by an opportunity to become a music pastor, I moved to **Guérard**, a small town in the Seine-et-Marne department, for a week. The week included three days of water fasting (a fast that allows water), to discover what the Man upstairs had to tell me about why I was put on Earth.
I had a lot of revelations including the fact that I need to delegate rather than taking everything on myself, but one passage of the Bible in particular attracted my attention. Isaac, Abraham's son, finds himself in a town called **Guerar**!!!

Incredible! I know nothing happens at random, but this is amazing, I didn't even realize there was a town called Guerar in the Bible!

Does your product meet your ideal client's expectations perfectly? If it does, then it's **your duty to do everything in your power to persuade them to buy your product**. If you don't, they will go on searching, and might never find the solution they want.

In one-to-one selling, **the client, not you, should be speaking 95% of the time**. Your questions should help them understand their situation and guide them toward making the right decision. Then you offer a solution by reformulating all their answers.

For example, let's say you're selling a couple's seminar. Here is **an example of conversation that you can reuse if you like**:

Your client: "Hello Sir, I saw your video, and I would like more details about your seminar."

You: "Hello, yes, of course. We have several products for couples, so could I ask you a few questions to find out what would be right for you?"

Your client: "Yes, of course."

You: "Great. Tell me a little bit about yourself."

Your client: "Well, I've been married for five years, we have a three-year-old boy, and because I work a lot, my wife complains that I'm not home enough. I tell her that we only have one salary coming in, because she stopped working when our son was born, and all of sudden so I took on the responsibility for all the general expenses, vacations, etc."

You: "OK. Does this cause conflict between you?"

Your client: "Yes, of course. She just doesn't understand that money does not grow on trees. That I do all this for her, and our child. If this seminar could help her understand that..."

You: "OK. How much do these conflicts at home affect you?"

I keep on reading and understand the parallels with my life. I must put my trust in Him more, because I'm going to have to get out of my comfort zone and take some risks, go much further.

One of the fundamental questions is: "**If I weren't paid to do this, would I do it anyway?**"

And then everything becomes clear. I understand that I'm not completely honest with all the people I work for, and that my main source of motivation is money. The same goes for Isaac, who was very rich because he inherited the fortune of his father Abraham.

Yet, he still lived in fear of not having enough. I too was afraid of going without. Are you frightened of not having enough? Do you know that there is no reason to be afraid and that you can, in just a single moment, decide that you actually have much more than you need?

Think about everything you have. Everything you've been through, where you are today. Nothing happens by accident, even the fact that you are holding this book right now. Everything is prepared in advance so you can live a life that is full of meaning: simple and happy. In abundance.

When I understood all that, my life changed. I took my responsibilities and **learned to say NO**. Regardless of the person or authority, I understand that I am the only person responsible for my life, and the only one I need to answer to is God.

I am so moved by that thought that I write a song that very same evening titled: "*Isaac's Blessing.*" So that I will never forget that revelation.

Your client: "Look, it got so bad that I don't even dare to go home in the evening, because at work nobody is constantly judging me. My colleagues understand me, and when we sometimes go out after work, we have a good time…"

You: "When you come home late, do you ever feel guilty?"

Your client: "Yes sometimes… But I really wish she would understand me…"

You: "I understand you. What is it that hurts you most in your relationship?"

Your client: "She is convinced that I don't love her, so, she threatens to leave me, and take our son with her! We are on the verge of separating actually…"

You: "Would you say your situation is now critical?"

Your client: "Definitely."

You: "All right. What would happen to you if your wife left you and took your son?"

Your client: "It would be terrible, I wouldn't survive! I need her and my son, they are my life!"

You: "How would you feel in that situation?"

Your client: "I would feel abandoned, rejected, just like when my father rejected me when I was young…"

You: "What would you feel physically? Would it affect your stomach, your throat?"

Your client: "My throat … and my stomach… I'd feel like I would suffocate… Alone in the dark…"

You: "Thank you for answering my questions, you've been very brave. I'll now ask you some more positive questions. Could you describe your ideal relationship?"

Your client: "Well, we would go away for weekend breaks as a family, once a month, to a different town. I'd play sports with my son. Maybe we could enjoy a romantic dinner once a week.

Is there anything more powerful than understanding that we have much more than we need right here, right now? Nothing can scare you because you already have everything. You can take any risk you like, you will always land on your feet.

So, one day I am researching how to change my life, I come across a blog, one list then another, I meet online marketers, I sign up for training courses, coaching, I travel around the world...

After another retreat, a little later, I meet a leader by the name of Claudiu who is offering a seminar that I register for without really knowing why.

It is game changing. The things this leader say strike me deep in my soul. He puts words to things I discovered about life, but at a much higher level of consciousness. I am not alone...

We become friends, I go to Ukraine with him for another four-day boot camp that transforms me to an even greater extent, and it is there that I put a permanent seal on **who I am and who I want to be**.

Everything makes perfect sense, and all the training courses I do have the same objective: being able to inspire others to achieve their mission.

My process is now clear, I start teaching it to the artists I coach at my singing school. In the meantime, I completely adapt it, and make it for people who want to become professional singers.

I bring in my new notions on self-confidence and the results are extraordinary.

We would find a hobby that we could do together. We would make love more often too. I would go home earlier to spend some time with my son, and talk to my wife."

You: "How else would you describe your ideal relationship?"

Your client: "We could go to Venice. She has always wanted to go there. It's incredibly romantic for her. I could also be more careful with my diet, and take up exercise again. I've put on a little weight. I can't stop myself. When I start eating, I just keep going. In fact, we could rekindle the relationship we had before..."

You: "How do you feel when you think about your ideal relationship with your wife?"

Your client: "I feel really good, like I'm flying, as though everything is still possible!"

You: "Can you feel something in your stomach, or in your throat?"

Your client: "No, I feel light, relaxed, as if a load has been taken away. Thank you very much for this conversation! I already feel much better!"

You: "It's my pleasure. What we have just done is a very small sample of what you will experience during the seminar entitled 'An Ideal Couple.' Could I describe how it could help you and your wife?"

Your client: "Yes, of course!"

You: "Thank you. With the help of the 'An Ideal Couple' seminar, you'll never have to make your wife understand that money does not grow on trees, your wife will never again complain when you come home late from work, you'll want to spend more time with your son, and talk to your wife. You will no longer feel like you're being judged, and your wife will finally understand you. She will no longer feel like you don't love her, and she will not threaten to leave and take your son with her anymore. You will no longer feel abandoned and rejected as you did by your father when you were young. You will not feel

Everyone isn't clear about their own values and vocation, because nobody has ever talked about them before.

I created a way of helping people to discover their mission of life!

I implement powerful online marketing strategies thanks to the first mastermind that I joined, I create a mastermind, but I'm still missing something that I can't put my finger on. My income goes up and down, and up and down again.

The years go by and I realize that every time I help a business person, I give them valuable advice that saves them a lot of time, or a lot of money.

I then discover a new mentor who lives in the United States, and who gives me the information I need for my business to really take off. I receive coaching for one day, and my vision of business shifts radically.

I come to realize that online marketing is just one of many possible business models, and that I have to tailor mine to my own personal profile. And then, everything falls into place. With my coach's help, I launch my new company **'Explosive Business'** which, within three months, shakes up my entire business, and enables me to hire an extremely efficient team which relieves me of the tasks that fall outside my expertise.

My income goes through the roof, and I'm suddenly faced with a challenge that only the rich experience. What should I do with all this money? I decide to give back a large part of it to an NGO: an association serving orphaned and impoverished children in Togo, to help them go to school, do their homework, eat a meal, and build more premises to accommodate the growing needs.

like you're being suffocated, or that you're alone in the dark anymore. You will finally be able to go out with your wife once a week, get out of town with your family for weekend getaways, play sports with your son, talk to your wife, or go on a romantic trip to Venice with her. You will also be able to lose weight, and rekindle the relationship you had before. And you will realize that anything is possible, you will feel like you are flying!"

Your client: "Wow, OK, uh, I'd like to sign up!"

You: "That's great news! You'll need your credit card with you to complete the transaction and confirm your registration. Let me know when you're ready."

Your client: "Just a second... All right, I'm ready!"

You: "Very good, the price of the two-day seminar is $1,995 per person. Would you also like to take part in the VIP day program?"

Your client: "OK, what is the VIP day?"

You: "You'll have special access to the coach who is an expert in relationship communication. You'll be able to ask them any questions you have, and you will be invited to go to a restaurant as a couple, and test out the principles that the coach has taught. Places are limited so if you'd like to save your spot, you'll need to decide now. I'm sure your wife will be pleased. What do you think?"

Your client: "Go on then, I'll go for the VIP day as well!"

You: "Great, that will be $1,000 more per person. Can you give me the numbers of your credit card please?"

Your client: "___ ___ ___ ___ ___ ___ ___, expiration date___ ___ and the last three digits on the back ____"

I know the founder personally. His school has the best exam results in the country. So, he has to create more and more classrooms to welcome the growing number of children.

If you want to support his association, AET, take a look at his website: http://avenirenfancetogo.org and tell him I told you about it.

I can now say that I am making a real contribution when I'm sent photos of children, buildings, and people doing the things they wanted to do.
I feel very proud, like I have achieved something important, because I finally get to experience the essence of what my parents wanted for me.

Here is a personal message for my parents:

Dad, thank you for teaching me to have the perseverance to reach the status I have today.
Thank you for instilling in me the desire to go beyond what I think I am capable of. Because I am no longer afraid of challenges, I am ready to meet them head on.
Thank you for being strict. Because I know how to control myself, I don't break the rules. I have respect for authority, including within my own company.
Thank you for helping me to set up this business that started off very small, because now we're reaping the benefits, and you had a part to play in that.
Thank you for believing in me over all these years, I know you don't talk much, but your actions speak volumes.
I am grateful for all that you have given up so that I could become the son who is standing in front of you today. **I love you.**

You: "Congratulations, you're now registered. You'll receive a confirmation email with all the details you need to book your hotel on site. Do you need more information?"
Your client: "No, thanks. That's great! I'm going to rush home and tell my wife. I can't wait to go, thank you very much. Bye!"
You: "Thank you, and see you soon, Sir."

Boom! Did you notice that at no point during the entire process we talked about the content of the seminar? That all we did was paraphrasing the client's pain and hopes, and serve them back to them on a platter?
Another point: Did you notice the emotional journey? **If the client cries, the sale is made.** If they are then filled with joy, they also agree to the **additional sale,** which is offered **each time** (the VIP day).

This example gives you the essence of a one-to-one sales discussion. It isn't exhaustive, but if you have your ideal client in front of you, on the phone, or by videoconference, it will be more than enough.

Your client decides with their emotions.

By using this method, I have been able to sell products ranging from $5,000, to several hundred thousands of euros. I think you should apply this method too.

Three final fundamental points:

1. Guarantee: You must reverse the risk, so, offer a money-back guarantee based on your ultimate gift to reassure the client. Even if that is not what motivates them to buy, it might help to close the sale.

Mom, thank you for teaching me that life isn't just about work. I have learned to stay with my family, and to nurture my friendships.
Thank you for showing me that I don't have to accept everything, and to say NO when something isn't right, so that I can respect myself.
Thank you also for knowing how to show your weaknesses, so that I could learn to show mine when something is beyond my control.
Thank you for making sacrifices so that I wouldn't be alone, or feel rejected when I was at my lowest point. **I love you.**

According to the ten commandments that God gives to Moses, if you **honor your parents you will be happy for the rest of your life**.

It took me years to understand that our parents can be a source of extraordinary wisdom, if we stop what we are doing, and really listen to them.

I hope you can do that. If you do not get along with your whole family, I hope you can reconcile with them all, because they are your roots, and a tree without roots does not survive for long.

You are like a tree, the deeper your roots, the longer your branches. You will be covered with lush green leaves and bear succulent fruit.

Trees are identified by the fruit they bear. I don't mean money, I think you realized that. Do you take care of the people who are close to you? What do they think of you, in your opinion?

I'd like to end day 6 with a few last words of advice. Then, in the coming days, we will take a look at the essential points you can review, starting with your health.

2. Price: Your rate must be high enough so that if you have five to ten clients a year, you can live comfortably. You won't have to wear yourself out finding them.

3. Additional sales: The best time to encourage a client to buy is when they are already making a purchase. Always have an additional sale opportunity ready. With that, you'll be able to double your margin! P.S. Why don't I talk about online marketing (landing pages, email campaigns, Facebook ads, etc.), since I use those on my websites? I have learned that **if you can't sell one-to-one, then you can't sell on a video. All web marketing experts are fantastic one-to-one salespeople. Here comes the summary**:

> **1. Elegant selling means asking questions based on the fears and aspirations of the client and then offering specific solutions based on their answers.**
>
> **2. If your product does not meet your client's expectations, don't sell it to them. Never force your client, seek only to help them.**
>
> **3. In elegant selling, the client should speak 95% of the time.**
>
> **4. Your client decides with their emotions. If your client cries, the sale is made.**
>
> **5. Always have a guarantee based on your ultimate gift.**
>
> **6. Set a high cost that covers your living expenses so that you only need to sell to five to ten clients a year.**
>
> **7. Always have an additional sale opportunity ready to double your margin.**

This day 6, which sums up my last seven years, has been deeply moving and upsetting to me. There have been many challenges, strong emotions, difficult decisions, changes of direction, sometimes accusations, and so on.

But I had to keep going, I have realized that the values my parents instilled in me fuel me and give me the energy I need for the journey.

If I could leave you with one piece of advice for a truly happy life, it would be this:

Honor your parents.

They won't be around forever, enjoy them to the fullest while they are alive, make peace with them. Wipe the slate clean, and start from scratch if you need to. You cannot change them, but you can change the way you perceive them.

Take care of your loved ones.

Your spouse and your children are the most important people in your life, never neglect them for a company, project, or job.

Work won't be by your side when you're on your deathbed, so give that some serious thought.

In the coming days, we'll go a little further into some fundamental topics...

You deserve the best.

Chapter 7: 20 Times More Money in One Month!

"Money is the answer to everything."
The Bible

Why 12 days? This is a reference to Tony Robbins's book, *Money: Master the Game,* which asks its readers a seemingly ordinary, yet, very powerful question.

Do you know how long it would take you to earn 1 million euros if you earned one euro per second? The answer is not easy, so I'll tell you: **it would take 12 days to earn 1 million euros**. Do you know how long it would take to earn 1 billion euros if you earned 1 euro per second? The answer is just as difficult to find: **it would take 32 years to earn 1 billion euros**.

The keys that I'm giving you in this book will help you to earn at least one million euros per year. I know that it will change your life, and if you take your life's mission seriously, you won't stop there, you'll be able to go even further.

There is a massive difference between a millionaire and a billionaire. **Millionaires change their own lives, but billionaires change the lives of millions more.**

So, if you think that money can't buy happiness, stay broke.
If you believe that all the rich people are selfish snobs, stay broke. However, **if you want to help the poor, then you should become very rich.** Earn at least 100 times more than the people you want to help, protect yourself, once and for all. The blind cannot lead the blind.

Day 7: The Formula for Life [13]

It's a new day of writing, and it begins on a rough note. According to some of the works by Dr. Filonov[14] (the only dry fasting specialist still alive today), there are several stages the body goes through during a dry fast.

There is a period during which the body temperature increases. Maybe that's what I am going through right now, because I feel hot on the inside, and cold showers, even if difficult to take, do me a world of good.

Honestly, this day is hard going, all I want to do is go to bed, drink three pints of ice-cold water one after the other, then juice, pints of juice, until I drown in a pool of juice...

But I have committed to this.

So, I go to bed (yes, I know). I feel uncomfortable. Time passes. It's one, two, and then four in the morning... The day has ended and I have not finished Chapter 7. Just too bad, I'll be behind schedule, but these things happen.

Of course, you must be wondering: **why put yourself through so much?**

You're right, I could have done what everyone else does: breathe, walk, eat, but I couldn't have called my book *12 Days* simply because I wrote it in 12 days. I needed another type of challenge.

---

[13] Watch the video for Day 7: http://12days.co/07

[14] Here is his website : filonov.net and you can use Google Translate (Russian site)

So, save yourself before trying to save others.

Learn how to play the money game without investing in it emotionally. If you lose a deal or if you find that you've been tricked, put it behind you. Don't take it personally. It's business. It's a jungle out there, and you need strong mental power.

Never use your business to do social work. Either you are doing business, which means bringing in a lot of money with your exciting AND lucrative offer, or you're doing social work with others and in that case, all you're looking to do is balance the books. But never do both at the same time. How many social entrepreneurs are billionaires in your opinion? None. Why not? For one very simple reason:

If you want to be a millionaire, you need to bill millionaires.

That's how I was able to multiply my cash flow by 20 in one month (from $7,819.72 to $152,364.45 if you want exact figures). The answer is easy and simple:

I changed my ideal client.

Before, I aimed my product at artists. And according to one of my mentors, artists are broke. Then I aimed at entrepreneurs. Boom! Same ultimate gift. New promise. New Star Offer. Nothing else. Are you getting the picture here?

Go for clients with money, not clients who are broke. Bring them what they don't have and want more than anything, and your bank account will skyrocket!

Here are just a few reasons:

- Few people know that I've been planning this book for a long time. It's not that I want to write this book to leave something of myself behind for posterity (though that would be great), and I'm not actually a fan of writing, I find it difficult, but **I have a duty to transmit**.
- If I don't finish this book **within 12 days**, I know that I won't take the time to finish it later, there will be corrections, proofreading, editing, that's for sure, but at least **the first draft will be finished**.
- It's a challenge and **I like challenges.** Although I am just starting out as an author, and had bad grades for literature in school, I want to prove that some belief systems can vanish in a flash, all you need to do is to act without paying attention to them.
- Because in terms of health, **I want to get rid of eczema** and a dry fast is the healthiest, most natural, most effective and fastest way to do that. I haven't tried colonic irrigation yet, but that's part of my plan for the coming weeks.
- I want to show the world that **food restriction is one of the simplest, most accessible ways to be healthier** and more energized. And it's free. People look for a miracle product, even though everything is inside our bodies, right here, right now.
- **I needed rest** in the countryside, and digestive rest is excellent for the body, and although it is not easy (especially mentally), my body is regenerating, and I'm experimenting with new things, like cold showers, for example.
- Because, although this book is primarily geared toward entrepreneurs, I want to reach out to anyone who is looking for the truth elsewhere, and **if I succeed in getting through to just one person, I will have been successful in what I set out to do**.

Now that we have clarified all that, let's talk about your finances. Most entrepreneurs are obsessed with sales revenue, but that's not actually the most important thing. The most important thing is your margin, the difference between your revenue and your expenses. Now things are getting interesting. But they are about to get better...

The money that is in your bank account: your cash flow. By adjusting your payment deadlines, you can pay in two months time and bring cash in yesterday. The more cash you have, the more financial power you have. Your cash is the first thing your bank manager looks at, and there is one basic thing that I have learned from my father:

Never get into trouble with your bank account.

Your bank manager is your most important creditor. If he or she freezes everything, you can't do anything. So if you have debts, you can stop payments to all other creditors, but never your bank manager. Always make sure you have cash in your bank account, and never exceed authorized overdraft deadlines, even if you have multiple accounts in different banks.

Now, before giving you an extremely powerful tool to manage and anticipate your cash flow, I must explain an important concept.

It is my belief that there are seven aspects of life:
1. Spirituality/Contribution
2. Physical and emotional health
3. Marriage/Children
4. Career/Business/Mission
5. Friends/Extended family
6. Personal finance
7. Leisure/Fun

Let me be very clear, do not do this without medical advice. However old you are.

So why am I doing it? Because I know my limits, I have been doing fasts for years, I have a vital force that helps me through them. I'm in the country, in a calm and healthy environment. There is also a personal and spiritual element to it, a search for truth so that I can share a profound message with you.

If you don't meet these criteria, then start by skipping breakfast, that's the easiest, because you already ate dinner the evening before. I think it's easier to skip breakfast than it is to skip dinner.

As soon as I start eating, it's harder for me to stop later during the day. So, I start eating as late as possible. I am usually eating one meal a day. I begin with fluids, such as vegetable juice.

I have a very high-quality juicer that processes raw fruit and vegetables that I would never have eaten otherwise. Like celery, spinach, chicory, etc. I mix them with apples, ginger, and turmeric.

It really quenches your thirst, especially when it comes straight from the juicer. Up until now, I drank very few juices, but after this fast, I'm really going to make the most out of them! You may be wondering what made me start eating in such a strange way.

If you eat the traditional three meals a day, I do understand that it must sound strange, so, I'll explain **why I decided to change my diet**.

Do this exercise: give yourself a score between 1 and 10 for each area, 1 meaning you are at an all-time low, and 10 meaning you are in paradise, you have reached perfection.
Example: If you are single without children, put zero for the marriage part.

As you have noticed, the Business and Personal Finance areas are separate.

You might have a well-functioning business, plenty of clients, great partnerships, and a very good salary, but in terms of personal finances, you might have a lot of expenses, pay a lot of taxes, or you may not optimize them, and so on.

The opposite is also true. Maybe your personal finances are working really well, you might have income from several sources, you can make money work for you, you may have inherited some, but on the other hand, your business isn't working out the way you'd like: you don't have enough clients, they fail to pay, or there may be bad supplier relationships, etc.

Whatever your situation is, read these next lines carefully.
I would like to clarify a few points about my approach.

You must understand that business is your best tool for growth and personal fulfillment, but **you must have multiple sources of income** to cover your personal expenses.

If your business is in bad shape, what will you say to your spouse? "Uh... Sorry honey...?"

Hmm... Doesn't quite cut it, does it?

More than a decade ago, while very busy doing music (concerts, classes, workshops, etc.), I carry a lot of heavy objects like mixing desks, speakers, 65-pound keyboards, etc.

I go home with a sore back, but I don't really pay much attention to it. I am young!

Except one day, I lean over to brush my teeth, and I am just stuck there, crushed under unbearable pain. I feel like I can barely breathe. I struggle to rinse my mouth, and like a little old man, I walk to bed with my back bent, and lie down without really having a clue what just happened. I am told it is lumbago. "Oh, isn't that something old people suffer from?" I take some medications, and go to the osteopath. It gets better, and then a few weeks later it happens again. I then consider buying a memory foam bed worth several thousands of dollars, the ones used by NASA...

Except that didn't solve the root cause of my problem. One day, I buy a book on back pain and then I understand that my posture, but also my diet, have an impact on my back. So, I look into it a bit more, and I realize that I could control my health way more than I thought.

Nothing is inevitable, **I don't have to suffer like this.** I have the means to prevent it. Another book on this subject has a huge impact on me: "We are alive so we must eat living food."[15] Wow! If you put it like this, it's obvious.

So, for ten days, I test a new eating habit based on fruit, vegetables and nuts.

---

[15] *Unlimited Power* by Tony Robbins

When you have got some personal cash together, ask yourself how this money can work for you. Seasonal rent real estate, stock market, wines, works of art, gold, cryptocurrencies? There are endless ways to make your money work for you, so find one, and apply it right away.

I suggest right now that you have:
1. Three months' worth of short-term savings, in case you cannot pay yourself for three months;
2. an amount set aside each month for the medium term in a locked account;
3. a monthly amount set aside for the long term in another locked account.

If you do this, you can protect yourself against unforeseen circumstances. This means that you must have a clear understanding of your expenses, and your personal income. And that's where a very powerful tool comes in...

This tool is better than a provisional budget because you can adjust it whichever way you like, and it is entirely related to **your bank account.** You can find out your balance ahead of time according to planned income and expenses, so you'll never be surprised again, and you will finally have PEACE. You can use it for your personal or professional finances. You track your financial data so you know in advance what your balance will be over the next months: if you can make a purchase or not, when you absolutely must cash in money from a client, the payment options to be negotiated with a supplier, your future revenue, any VAT that needs to be paid, taxes, etc.

You should use this tool to control your personal and professional cash flow, otherwise you are headed right for financial suicide!

My friends and family are afraid, they tell me that I am going to die, that they don't want me to pass out.

What is amazing is that I do not experience any discomfort. I actually had much more energy! I climb the stairs much faster and don't get out of breath. I have a flat stomach, I walk, I feel supple, light, quick, and intellectually speaking, my brain is working fast. I am lucid. Strangely, my weight drops without me wanting to, it is simply a collateral effect. So, I continue the experiment and **I lose 22 pounds in 3 weeks**. Most people would be afraid of that, but I feel at the top of my shape.

I understand the merits of these principles, so I decide to apply them in my own way. I no longer buy animal products, but when I'm invited to dinner, I eat whatever I'm served. The next day, I go back on my diet. I continue my research, and I come to understand that the three-meal-a-day cycle isn't necessary either, and that only one meal can be enough, and helps to detoxify and eliminate the waste that has accumulated in the body.

So, I cut out breakfast, it doesn't bother me too much because in the meantime, I have done several fasts: long, short, water or dry, and my dependence on food (because that's what it is) has decreased gradually.

Quick note: I forgot to say that more than a decade ago, I had an extremely poor diet. "Vegetable" was a rude word for me. I wouldn't touch fruit. I ate kebabs, cheeseburgers with bacon and fries, pizzas and big rice dishes with a ton of peanut sauce...

Let me explain the abbreviations so you can understand:

B = Balance / R = Revenue / T = Total / E = Expense

	Jan	Feb	Mar	Apr	May	Jun	Jul	Aug	Sep	Oct	Nov	Dec	T
B	30	20	50	40	20	40	20	0	-10	-30	30	80	
R	60	60	30	50	110	20	70	20	60	110	140	250	
T	90	80	80	90	130	60	90	20	50	80	170	330	
E	20	10	5	40	30	10	30	5	30	15	30	50	
E	15	5	25	20	40	5	40	15	30	15	40	40	
E	35	15	10	10	20	25	20	10	20	20	20	30	
T	70	30	40	70	90	40	90	30	80	50	90	120	
B	20	50	40	20	40	20	0	-10	-30	30	80	210	

You have perhaps noticed that the balance from the end of January is taken up again at the beginning of February, but also that in August and September you need to plan for increased cash income otherwise the overdraft will be used more than two months in a row.

You won't miss any details with this tool, and above all, you can update it, modify it, make simulations, etc.

In the **Explosive Business** program, you can get all your dashboards fully configured, so you know exactly where you are and where you are going. If you want to apply, visit our website: http://explosivebusiness.com

So, as you understand, I've come a long way. My former eating habits were slowly but surely leading me to diabetes, colon cancer and other unpleasantness.

Remember that I am no better, and in reality, much worse than you in many areas, just ask my friends and family!

I used to be able to finish two kebabs in a row! So, I wouldn't dare think of preaching to you. What matters to me is your health.

The purpose of this book is to simply show you that it is possible for your life to be what you deserve it to be, despite your faults.

Nothing can and should prevent you from fulfilling your dreams, because the seed that will allow you to find all the solutions to the problems you will encounter is right there inside you.

Your most important WHY will lead you to victory!

I suggest three solutions that you can combine whichever way you like:

1. Eat 80% raw organic fruits and vegetables, in juice form which is easier, even though it does take a little time to prepare.
2. Eat two or even just one meal a day, and dry fast in between if possible.
3. Try short fasts, lasting one to three days without water if possible, if your health allows it and if your doctor agrees with it.

Now it's time for the summary!

1. If you want to help the poor, you need to become at least 100 times richer than they are.

2. If you want to be a millionaire, you need to bill millionaires.

3. Never get into trouble with your bank account.

4. You must have several sources of income other than your business.

5. Use a dashboard for your bank account to anticipate your personal and professional cash flow and your mind will be at PEACE.

Let's get back to where we were, I kept on investigating and came up with an extremely simple and powerful formula that allowed me to stay aware of the energy of life that lies within us.

You may not believe me, but it is a version of what Dr. Arnold Ehret recommends in his book *Health and healing through fasting*.

This formula for life is very simple and explains a lot about how our lifestyle affects our health.

I'll leave you to take a look, and think about it:

LIFE = Breathing - Food

Chapter 8: Focus!

"Keep your eyes on the finish line, and not on the turmoil around you."
Rihanna

This chapter is the densest in the book. If you haven't understood the ideas in the other chapters, now is the time to go back over the summaries, then over the chapters if you haven't put them into practice yet.

This book is a manual, it isn't a novel. Apply, apply, and apply again. Everything works, and I have purposely taken out all the superfluous details so that the process can be simple and quick.

How can you keep your focus and not get distracted in the 21st century? Every effort is made to divert our attention from our ultimate goal, so, it is essential to put safeguards in place, to have powerful habits that keep your feet on the ground, while still keeping your mind connected to Heaven.

1. One of the biggest factors for interruptions is the cellphone. I was a geek in the past, I know this all too well. So, after much thinking, negotiating, failures, and changing phones, I made a radical decision:

I no longer own a cellphone.

Of course, you do not have to go to this extreme, but simply turning off your phone when you are in a meeting, with your family, or at the office and doing a very important task, will help you stay 100% focused.

2. **Do not answer your emails**
Delegate email management to an assistant who will come get to you.

Day 8: 1, 2, or 5 Talents?[16]

After a difficult seventh day, I am determined to make up for lost time and to write everything I have planned to write for today. The mission is important because chapters 7 and 8 are packed full of information, and I hope you have a clear understanding of the principles I am giving you.

Obviously if you are an experienced entrepreneur, all this may seem trivial, but it is always beneficial to get a reminder of the basics. I am currently working while listening to inspirational movie soundtracks, and I feel more productive.

This part is more difficult to write because I have to match up with the opposite chapter, and that's a good thing, because it pushes me to my limits.

I feel much better today, I was able to make a clay poultice to apply to my eczema, and it worked well. Of course, I had my cold shower, which still feels just as satisfying, even though I came out frozen.

Dr. Filonov recommends doing dry fasts near mountainous areas where the air is cool and clean, and where there are waterfalls. I understand perfectly what he means about waterfalls because the shower head is my waterfall!

The ritual I use before each 25-minute session is effective and allows me to refocus on the "why" in this book.

I have emotional ups and downs, but I'm holding up.

---

[16] Watch the video for Day 8: http://12days.co/08

with important information about your VIP clients or the prospects you are currently tracking.

With these first two tips, you can boost your concentration a lot, but that is not all.

3. **Work for two hours a day**

You didn't expect that one! If you only had two hours a day to spend working, which tasks would you focus on? What would be the most important?

Personally, I use the site http://marinaratimer.com (I'm using it right now) to work according to the Pomodoro method, so I work in 25 min , then take a 5 min break, then 25 min work, then 5 min break, etc.

This site is excellent because it allows you to use the usual method or to configure any other type of timer. I use the traditional Pomodoro method and I make myself follow the notifications and stop when it rings, and start up again when it rings again. So, as soon as I launch it, I'm set for two hours of non-stop work, and I can really concentrate.

Try it just once, with no interruptions, and you'll see what I mean!

4. **Surround yourself with a team of champion**

You might tell me that it's not easy to find great people. In fact, it is, but you have to look hard, you have to offer good pay, great reasons to leave their current position (they often already have jobs), offer genuine development prospects, and a big project for them to take on. Champions must always be stimulated, they should never be left to rest on their laurels. Nothing must be easy for them.

I believe that the first position to fill is the Super Assistant who can

When this book comes out, I will be delighted to say:
"I did it!"

It is strange, that feeling of going so long without anything to eat or drink, yet to be able to continue functioning normally. I'm going beyond the limits of what is acceptable to most humans, and it is actually not that much of a struggle.

Sure, it does require some stamina, but it's not like I'm all alone in the middle of the desert. I can eat if I really need to, I have as much to drink as I like, everything I could need is right there for the taking.

But this feeling of lightness, this empty stomach that is looking flatter and flatter, these very thin arms and legs, this mind in perfect working order... Do we really know the human body? Have we really studied its endless possibilities, or are there still mysteries about it? It is possible for anyone to stop eating a little, for one day, then for two, and so on. Regardless, I am having one of the most memorable experiences of my life, and I will do whatever I can to share it, even though I know it won't have any medical value.

The fear of going without... Would I be so at ease if I didn't have provisions within my reach? I honestly don't know. Abundance is a state of mind that we all need to be aware of. I was born into abundance, and so were you. Even if you believe you have nothing, you actually have everything you need, here and now.

Do I sound like a crazy fool? Fine, no big deal. I am actually healthy, both in body and in mind. I'm happy to be myself, whatever people think of me. Now, I'd like to tell you a story...

eventually become your managing director: the person who basically runs the company when you're not there. Your right-hand man or woman, in whom you have complete trust. Even when you're not around, you know that **the company will be flourishing**.

You need an Administrative Assistant who will handle official documents, filing, invoice payments, accounts, etc.

Then you need to find an excellent Salesperson who was born to sell, and who likes challenges, a hunter who will earn great commission on each sale.

Then consider taking on a Quality Manager who will create and apply the right procedures so that each new person can work and follow the company approaches without question.

For all the positions you fill, you need people who are **passionate AND excellent,** but also flexible people who will tailor themselves to your business, your culture, and overall vision. If not, they have no reason to be a part of your business.

Later you can hire a marketing manager who will set up all the internet sales funnels to encourage your prospects to buy.

And finally, find someone who can help you, or even replace you as you deliver your skills. In order to spend time out of your business, **you are going to have to learn to clone yourself**.

Tread carefully here, because champions are not always easy to detect straightaway, and sometimes the opposite happens, you think you have found a champion and it turns out they are not what you thought they would be. So, test them on small tasks first, and then increase their responsibilities while giving them the freedom to move forward, whichever way they like.

"A man was about to set off on a journey, but first summoned his servants to him and entrusted them with his possessions while he was gone.

He gave five talents to one, two to another, and one to the third, each according to his potential, and then he left immediately.

The one who had received five talents went off to work with them, and earned five more talents.

The man who had received the two talents also earned two more.

The man who had received only one talent went to dig a hole in the ground, and hid his master's talent.

After a long time, the master returned from his trip and asked the servants to give an account of how they had used the money.

The one who had received five talents came forward with five others, and said: 'Master, you gave me five talents. Here are five more that I have earned.'

His master said to him: 'Well done, my good and faithful servant; you have been loyal in handling this small amount, so now I will give you much more. Come and share in your master's joy.'

The servant who had received two talents also came forward and said: 'Master, you gave me two talents. Here are two more that I have earned.'

His master said to him: 'Well done, my good and faithful servant; you have been loyal in handling this small amount, so now I will give you much more. Come and share in your master's joy.'

The servant who had received only one talent then came forward and said: 'Master, I knew you were a harsh man, harvesting crops you didn't plant and gathering crops you didn't cultivate.

I was afraid I would lose your money, so I hid it in the ground. Look, here is your money back.'

His master replied: 'You are a wicked and lazy servant, you knew that I harvested crops I didn't plant and gathered crops I didn't cultivate. So, you should have deposited my money in the bank, and when I came back at least I would have gotten some interest on it.

5. Stick to a powerful morning ritual

I've tested dozens, but the most powerful is one created by Hal Elrod, the author of *Miracle Morning*. His ritual is called SAVERS:

S for Silence/Meditation/Prayer
A for Affirmations
V for Visualization
E for Exercise
R for Reading
S for Scribing

The idea is to spend the same time on each step, so that you work on your body, soul and mind. Here's the great advice that he gives **if you have very little time in the morning**.

Do the one-minute version for each letter, so the **whole ritual** will take you **just six minutes**!

Can you honestly say you don't have six minutes? Even when I'm running late, I do it anyway because I know that it has a huge impact on my day. So now there are no more excuses!

6. Eat one meal, every evening

Drink vegetable or fruit juice during the day to keep your energy levels up, and stay hydrated.

You need to understand that digestion saps 70% of your energy, so if you want to feel energized all day long (if you can't work for only two hours each day), don't eat until you come to the end of your workday. You could even eat some raw fruit and vegetables if you feel that you really must chew on something.

It is as simple as that.

Take the money from this servant, and give it to the one with ten talents.
To those who use well what they are given, even more will be given, but from those who do nothing, even the little they have will be taken away.
Now throw this useless servant into outer darkness, where there will be weeping and gnashing of teeth.'"

I have a question for you: what kind of servant are you? The one with 5 talents, 2 talents or 1 talent?

The one with 5 talents had to work hard to obtain 5 more talents. The one with 2 talents had to work hard to obtain 2 more talents. The one who had 1 talent hid it, out of fear, laziness, or spite.

Result: They started out with 5-2-1 and finished up at 11-4-0 (with a severe punishment for the third servant).

There is an exponential dimension here as well.

This parable shows that **it's not the cards you hold that matter, but what you do with them.**

The servants with five and two talents put what they had to good use, and received praise from their master **without being compared to each other**. There is nothing in the parable that suggests they didn't have to struggle, fight, overcome difficulties, etc.

But **they persevered**.

One of my mentors says: "If you are born broke, it's not your fault. If you die broke, it's 100% your fault."

7. Persevere until you succeed

It sounds trite, but you need to understand that life is not linear, but exponential. When you look at the growth of all the companies that have seen spectacular results over the course of several years, all have grown exponentially.

That's how everything works in nature. You plant a seed and you have nothing for years, then one day there is a stem, a trunk, then leaves, then fruit.

So, never look for results right away unless you have already created several businesses in the past. If you keep this in mind, you will always ask the right questions before following a particular strategy, because you will know that if you want to see results, you have to keep at it for a long time.

Now let's recap that advice:

---

1. Turn off your cellphone, or simply get rid of it.

2. Don't answer your own emails: delegate them to your assistant who knows what to pass on to you.

3. Work for two hours each day to force yourself to be very effective: apply the Pareto principle to the extreme.

4. ONLY hire champions, based on their attitude first, then passions and excellence.

5. Use the powerful six-minute **SAVERS morning ritual**.

6. Eat one meal a day in the evening, because of digestion, to keep your energy intact throughout the day.

7. Persevere until you succeed, because growth is always exponential, never linear.

Here is another important truth from this parable:

More talents = More responsibilities

It's great to have plenty of resources, but that also means a great deal of responsibility.

An entrepreneur is responsible for his resources.

Now that you have these keys, what kind of servant are you going to be?

1, 2, or 5 talents?

Chapter 9: Stop!

"Whenever you want to, you can withdraw into yourself. Nowhere can man find a quieter or more untroubled retreat than in his own soul."

Marcus Aurelius

The worst thing possible, whether you are successful or struggling, is not knowing when to stop. We are all constantly caught up in the noise of technology, and the abuse of information around us. None of this helps us to make the best decisions for our life, and for our businesses.

The best thing to do is to take some time out, go away for a week (or more) to get closer to nature, somewhere that inspires you, and rest. And I'm not talking about "holidays," those times when we travel somewhere visiting countless places that we won't even remember. Nor am I talking about the times when you stand in line for two hours with hundreds of other tourists just like you, to experience an attraction that lasts for just three minutes.

Three basic rules define true rest:

1. **Physical rest**: lying down, because there is nothing better than that position; it is the only one where the body doesn't need to support the back, so remember that point the next time your doctor tells you to rest.

2. **Mental rest**: don't try to change the world with your ideas, or mull over past or present worries. In fact, the best thing for the mind is for you to put in some earplugs and go to sleep, that's when the body has the best opportunity to restore itself completely.

3. **Digestive rest:** in other words, dry fasting (without water) or water fasting (with water). Treat your digestive system to a rest, it has been working for you constantly for decades...

Day 9: The Secret Behind the Secret[17]

I'm starting to understand why my body enjoys cold water so much. I think my core body temperature is high, because I feel "hot." As weak and diseased cells burn themselves, they must increase the body's overall temperature.

My tongue is incredibly white, which according to fasting specialists, is quite normal. My heart is beating rather fast, but everything is fine, I don't feel weak at all. I rinse my mouth thoroughly, then brush my teeth with bicarbonate of soda. It's less unpleasant than usual, I keep some water in my mouth to dilute it and rub gently. I think I'll use that technique again in the future.

It feels like the plaque on my teeth is disappearing, and that my teeth are whiter. I splash some water on my face, and it brings about the same feeling as the cold shower, so much so that I don't wipe it off. Anyway, it's so hot out at the moment that it doesn't stay wet for long. I also think that my skin is absorbing as much water as it can from the outside.

As my hands are cold, I place them on my skull to continue this cooling sensation. I hold a little water inside my mouth, I think about this idea of waiting for the outside water to stay in my mouth before swallowing. This idea of not swallowing right away is also related to the constant sensation of lack...

When you eat or drink, how long do you hold what you have inside your mouth? One second, three? Apart from wine experts who go on to spit out what they are tasting, very few people take the time to really appreciate what they have in their mouth for three to five minutes.

Your body will at last find all the energy it needs to repair, optimize, and build up everything it needs so that you are in your best shape to channel all your energy into your usual activity.

---

17 Watch the video for Day 9: http://12days.co/09

These three laws apply systematically, and to all people. You can, of course, replace water with vegetable juice, but avoid solid foods as much as you can for a while.

Here are some advantages to getting this type of total rest (related to dry fasting) according to Dr. Filonov:

- Removal of cysts, hernias, endometriosis, ulcers, asthma, arthritis, fibroids, etc.;
- 80% increase in the immune system;
- Removal of benign tumors in the breast, and of adenomas of the prostate;
- Rejuvenation and prolongation of life expectancy;
- Healing of radioactive radiation (see Chernobyl), prevention of cancer;
- Improvement of the five senses, intuition and libido.

There are plenty of others, but I'll stop there in the hope that you have been sufficiently convinced.

The purpose of a retreat is to help you review your life, and find out if you are still going in the right direction. It's like taking a break at a highway rest stop. Every two hours is best.

Do you do that?

How can you be absolutely certain that you are not driving in the wrong direction, or that you have taken the right exit? Sometimes stress forces us... Forces us to make quick decisions and we don't realize the extent of the consequences until much later.

Yet if we did that, we would enjoy our food and drinks more, and eat less of it.

There is a real science known as therapeutic chewing, which involves chewing up and down 100 times for each bite before swallowing.
Dr. Fletcher identified this technique and used it on himself and many of his patients. Countless cases of obesity have been reversed, simply by using this slow chewing technique. When you chew slowly, the brain has time to evaluate the composition of the food, and can adjust the acidity of the saliva and various digestive juices. When the feeling of satisfaction comes, you aren't tempted to eat anymore. Some people call it "mindful eating." Taking the time to taste and smell each flavor, each texture, making sure it is completely pureed (like babies) before slowly allowing the mixture to move down into your esophagus. By doing that, you take care of your body so it can do the rest of the work.

Obviously, this is all common sense, but as you are aware, knowing things is simply not enough. You have to experience them within your body so that they come to life, and you create a new habit. Think about it next time you eat, chew your food 100 times, it's good for your health.

This will be my mission on the 13th day: to take the time to enjoy my first glass of water. I'll spend 15 minutes drinking a glass of water, so that the water gently mixes with my saliva, and then I'll swallow it slowly. It requires self-control. Will that be more difficult than 12 days of fasting? I don't know. It is often said that the recovery period is more important than the fast itself. There is apparently a rejuvenating effect as well, I can't wait to see how my friends and family react! Anyway, today is a peaceful day. I have written two thirds of this

In our Rock Star Entrepreneur programs, we reduce our clients' workloads so much that they have the time and energy to do the most important thing in their business:

DECIDE.

This is the essence of the leader, his or her ability to decide, to say yes or no, to go in one direction and not another, to refuse an opportunity to conform, to stay the course whatever happens, even though things may look bleak.

Entrepreneurs don't think in terms of time, but of results. They want their result, whether that result takes 40 seconds or 40 years to achieve. So, their ability to decide, after taking into account all the advice from their team, is fundamental.

Some of your decisions can have a huge impact on your business, so here are three questions that a US entrepreneur named Stu McLaren asks himself before making a decision:

- Am I making a profit?
- Am I contributing?
- Does it lower my stress level?

You may have noticed that these three questions are fairly similar to the three conditions required for a Star Offer...

The equation always involves a win-win.

book, and I still have some amazing advice to share with those of you who are tenacious enough to still be reading. So here is an extra gift, hidden in this emotional introspection section.

You must BE before you can DO.

Yes, you've heard it before, especially if you're a regular at seminars or training courses, or if you read books on personal development or leadership. So, I will go into a bit more detail here.

If you can't feel the essence of what you want deep in the inner fibers of your being, don't try to make it happen. You must feel it, yes, but you must also have **complete belief in what you're doing before you start doing it**.

If you don't, if you approach something nervously, which might not necessarily be a bad thing in itself, it may very well hinder your chances when you are trying to sell your new product at 10 or 100 times the price you usually sell it at. The other person will sense your anxiety, and it will compromise the sale.

This is where the Affirmations and Visualization stages of Hal Elrod's morning ritual come into play. **To affirm means to proclaim a belief with strength, determination, and total conviction; to be convinced that it is the only possibility**. You shout a battle cry that can be heard far and wide!

Whether you think you can or you think you can't, you're right. This quote is from Henry Ford: there can be no result without conviction! To persuade others, you must be persuaded yourself! If you are "so-so, we'll see, maybe, maybe not," your guaranteed result is: **ZERO INCOME**.

Is that clear?

Well! Here we are already at the summary of the chapter:

---

1. It's vital to rest if you want to optimize your health.

2. There are three laws of rest that you need to follow:

- Physical rest (lying down);
- Mental rest (sleeping);
- Digestive rest (fasting).

3. DECIDING is the most important role for an entrepreneur

4. Here are the three questions to ask yourself to make the best decisions:

- Am I making a profit?
- Am I contributing?
- Does it lower my stress level?

Second part: the visualization that comes immediately afterward. Close your eyes and feel your emotions, experience, hear, touch your life, and be grateful for what you have already achieved. **Faith is the demonstration of the things we hope for.** Nothing else matters when you begin to imagine it.

Affirmation and visualization are the two most powerful ways to anchor a new truth within your soul.

You can also write or record set phrases, we'll talk about them again in the next day.

Chapter 10: What Is Essential to You?

"Treasure love for your family, love for your spouse, love for your friends..."

Steve Jobs

These are the last words uttered by Steve Jobs before he died. You can't take your wealth or your awards with you when you die, so be aware of what is essential to you if you don't want to be alone, both now and when you are lying on your death bed.

Balance doesn't exist.

We are either on one side or on the other. Like a captain at the helm of a ship sailing on the water, this is real life.

Most people try to balance their personal and professional lives as if they were two opposing forces. It actually is a matter of priorities. Here's what I have learned from my parents, Steve Jobs and many other people who have a lot more life experience than me:

Your marriage and your family life are more important than your career.

Boom! No negotiations. One of the reasons I do not have a cellphone is that I don't want to be interrupted by business concerns when I'm at home. All it would take is to just forget to turn it off, and there it would be, a notification, a brief email, a client emergency, and so on. In my experience, professional emergencies do not exist. Even though my biggest million-dollar client may be clamoring for a promise we have not delivered, **I remain unreachable**.

Day 10: Your Statement of Confidence[18]

Today it is very easy to get up, so easy that I make a 15-minute video outside and then take a walk into the fresh air until I find a stream. I would have enjoyed swimming in it, but unfortunately, the water didn't seem to be too clean.

Then, when I get back, I take a cold shower, shave, and watch some videos on water quality: how to purify it, the benefits of clay, seawater, and so on.
I even try distilling water on my own. Despite my efforts, my experiment is inconclusive. All the same, I'll drink what I have tried distilling in three days as planned.

Otherwise, I'll use my big plastic bottle of mineral water (my distiller has been ordered and should arrive next week) to start off, with a little green clay if there is anymore left by then, because I still have to prepare the poultice for my eczema (which is actually going away slowly, but surely).

After all my purchases, I decide to write the very short chapter 10 as well as Day 10 entries, in which I talk about your **STI: Statement of Trust and Intent**.

But before that, I must explain two opposing factors that may create confusion, especially among those who live by the law of attraction.

There exists two dimensions: **the visible reality** that everyone knows, and **the invisible truth** that no one else but you know.

---

[18] Watch the video for Day 10: http://12days.co/10

However, if I received a call from a hospital because one of my friends or family had been in an accident that would be a real crisis, and work would vanish instantly.

So, cherish your wife (go on a date with her every week), your children (organize play dates with them), your friends or extended family (parents, cousins, aunts, uncles).

Take care of those who really matter, and give them priority. Do not pretend, stay in touch with them, write special dates in your diaries, plan regular meetings, put systems in place, because it's too sad to lose touch with someone you love because of the routine.

Make a list of your loved ones and decide how often you want to hear from them, and how you wish to contact them (visits, invitations, parties, videoconferences, telephone, instant messages, etc.). Then act on it.

Chapter summary (yes, this one is very short):

---

1. Balance doesn't exist. There are only priorities.

2. Your marriage and your family life are more important than your career.

3. Set up a system to keep in touch with the loved ones that you have listed.

In your imagination, **you must visualize and proclaim the invisible so that your actions bring it to reality.**

That means your subconscious must believe that it is true right now so that it does not sabotage you when you actually move in that direction. That's why you have to repeat it **tirelessly and with POWER**, and be completely certain before you take any action.

If not, it won't work. So, if you change how you are (your way of thinking or mindset), you'll change your outcomes.

In practice, this statement is a small series of short and powerful sentences that affirm what you are in your invisible truth.

Examples: I am an outstanding coach.
I make $10 million in sales revenue each year.
I have complete confidence in myself.

Create your STI and integrate it into your morning SAVERS ritual.

This truth will become real and visible in a short time.

You will have extraordinary power and conviction.

Chapter 11: Are You Ready to Change the World?

"If a man has not discovered something that he will die for, he isn't fit to live."

Martin Luther King

What is your fight? What do you want to stop in the world? Being successful in business, and having a happy personal life is all well and good, but what cause would you be willing to die for?

As long as you don't have the answer to that question, your life is useless.

Do you only want to be living tissue? Just one more human who nurtures the existing system, and then dies, like 97% of the population? Or do you want your life to make a difference? Do you want it to have a significant impact on the lives of millions of other people?

Because it's what you want, you're going to have to pick sides. As I told you in Chapter 7, becoming a millionaire (in 12 days)[19], isn't that hard if you follow the advice in this book, and it is guaranteed if you join one of our **Explosive Business** programs.

But becoming a billionaire (in 32 years) in order to change the lives of millions of people, means dedicating your life to that cause, it means coming up against obstacles from lobbies, lawsuits, breaches of contract, theft, corporate spies, journalists who write hateful articles about you, the list goes on…

Find your cause and get ready to fight for the next 40 years of your life.

---

[19] See Chapter 7

Day 11: One Last Detail[20]

I didn't mention it, but at the end of day 10, while I was brushing my teeth, I saw a small winged animal a little different from the mosquitoes, flies, wasps and butterflies that I sometimes come across... **A bat!**

AAAAAAAAAAAAAAAAAAAAAAAAAAAAAAAAAAAHHHHHHHHH!!!
Yes, I know, authors don't usually write that in a book, but bats aren't pretty, they fly around everywhere and most of all, <u>no bats were mentioned in the contract!</u>

So here, on the one hand, we have, a frightened little bat, who is much more afraid than I am, and on the other, a tall strapping man measuring 6'1", running like a three-year-old child being chased down by a huge Doberman...

It's ridiculous, I know, especially that it can't get out, and dawn is breaking, since it's a nocturnal creature, it will soon be looking for a hideout...

So, I calm down, open the lower windows, turn off the lights, and go to bed, hoping it won't fall on top of me while I'm fast asleep. (What an idea!) And then I fall asleep.

I don't see any sign of the bat the next day. I mention it to the landlord, who isn't thrilled that it was inside the house, but suggests that I leave the windows opened, hoping that it'll get out in the evening. So that's what I do. And then at around 9:30 pm, it comes down again and starts flying around as it had the day before. Meanwhile, I used Luc Geiger's NERTI protocol to get rid of my unconscious fears.

---

[20] Watch the video for Day 11: http://12days.co/11

So, after all that you'll be genuinely proud of yourself, because you will have become a History Maker, like Mother Theresa, Michael Jackson, Walt Disney, Gandhi, Steve Jobs, Martin Luther King, Abraham Lincoln, Nelson Mandela, etc.

Whatever is your area of expertise, you have exceptional power right there in your hands, and that's the power to **create your own contribution, here and now.**

Now take a pen, and write down what you would really like to change about the world, something that disturbs you deep in your guts, something very specific that has had an impact on your own life.

Here are some examples: education for young people living in underprivileged areas in French-speaking countries, how the homeless are managed in large European cities, protection for women who are victims of domestic abuse in North Africa, etc.

Begin your sentence with: "I want to eradicate/change/create ... in the world." Fill in the blank.

Now it is time for our summary:

> **1. If you have not discovered a cause you are willing to die for, your life is useless.**
>
> **2. Find your cause by dedicating the next 40 years of your life to it. You'll need to become a billionaire to make it happen.**
>
> **3. Whatever your field, you can contribute here and now.**
>
> **4. Create your sentence: I want to [change] ... in the [world].**

So now that I'm more relaxed, I can see the bat looking and looking... then finding its way out!

Then it comes back, "Oh my God!" Finally, it gets out and doesn't come back, and then I close ALL the windows. Yes!

That's all well and good, but it distracts me from one last detail that I need to share with you so that you are completely free as you start out on your journey to becoming a rich entrepreneur who is happy and proud of themselves.

Have you forgiven the people who have hurt you?

Grudges, anger, and a desire for revenge are poisons, milestones around the neck, and burdens that chain you to your past, and prevent you from moving forward in many different areas.

You may have settled some things, but I'm talking about **total forgiveness**. You wipe the slate clean and never look back.

As soon as you are ready, stand in front of a mirror, and imagine that the person is in front of you. Tell them what you would like to tell them, in complete honesty (and remember to forgive them, obviously).

If you do this sincerely, an enormous weight will be removed from your shoulders, and you will feel much lighter.

Forgiveness quickly releases you from sufferings.

Take this very seriously, I assure you, it really works.

Chapter 12: The Ultimate Secret

"You cannot self-criticize and be generous; when you know how to bounce back after an error, everything becomes possible."
Eric BEHANZIN

That's what I have taught my singers for years. Some piano or guitar learners used to say: "Wait, I went wrong, I'm going back to the beginning again." I would answer: "Oh really? When you get on a train, but find yourself in the wrong train carriage, do you ring the alarm for you to get in the right one?" They, of course, understand that you simply have to keep moving with the train.

You need a big ego to stay fixated on your mistakes. It takes a lot of work. But forgetting about them and moving on requires focus, not on yourself, but on your audience, on your client, who may not even have noticed the expert's mistake.

If you never make mistakes, you're not going fast enough.

Facebook brings out innovations and makes mistakes, Google and even Apple make mistakes... What about you? Do you know this proverb?

Fail forward.

It means make mistakes now. Because in doing so, you will learn so much that when you are in an important position, nothing will scare you, and you will have learned plenty of lessons from your past mistakes.

Day 12: A Happy Ending?[21]

"He who conceals a transgression seeks love." The Bible

It's a new day, and the very last one. I get up to go for a stroll at around 7 am, and walk barefoot through the cool grass of the forest. I feel the dew on the soles of my feet, it is wonderful...

Now, I like the cold. Which is pretty crazy, since I must have lost about twenty pounds. I like to feel the coolness of the wind go through me, despite my shivering, it makes me feel alive.

I am now sure I could go on much longer. It takes a little time to get used to it, I need to sort out this mouth detoxification issue which is bothering me, but I'm going to keep on with a liquid fast for at least a week. I'm going to be drinking fruit and vegetable juices over the next few days. I don't really feel like eating anything solid. I may eat some very juicy and refreshing fruit such as melons or watermelons, but nothing too sweet.

I usually crave seeds and nuts, but I don't feel like eating those at all, even though I have them at hand. I'm not tempted at all, so I won't touch them. Through this 12-day dry fast, life has taken on a new dimension. I know what is possible and I know that when my mind decides, my body follows.

Embrace the pain.
... About pain, I talk about perfectionism in Chapter 12, a way of working that is supposed to protect us.

---

[21] Watch the video for Day 12: http://12days.co/12

But to do so, you need to be clear on one basic idea: toss your perfectionism away and just be yourself.

Own your spelling mistakes, your bad jokes, your choice of logos, your strategic decisions. **STOP CENSORING YOURSELF**.

Do you wish to do something in line with your vision? Do it. That's how I ended up writing this book. I repeat, it isn't perfect, but it is done.

Perfectionism creates procrastination.

You will never be ready anyway, so ACT NOW. There is only one way to make this happen, and it's on the right-hand page of Day 12. **Give, give again, and keep on giving**.

The ultimate secret is how quickly you can implement what you do: the sooner you act, the faster you'll be rich.

We've arrived at our last summary in the book.

---

1. If you never make mistakes, you're not going fast enough. STOP CENSORING YOURSELF.

2. Perfectionism creates procrastination.

3. Give, give again, and keep on giving.

4. The ultimate secret is how quickly you can implement what you do: the sooner you act, the faster you'll be rich.

We use perfectionism to protect ourselves against our own mistakes. Why do we do that?

We don't forgive ourselves for our past mistakes.

It's understandable if you have made mistakes and the consequences have caused your sufferings. But forgive yourself for it all now.

Remember the Absolute Master of Forgiveness, the one who suffered it all, even though He was innocent.

Jesus Christ said: "Forgive them, for they know not what they do."

The essence of love is forgiveness.

Look at yourself in the mirror, and do the same exercise, talk to yourself honestly.

When the relief comes, be grateful to yourself, to your loved ones and to Him, because He has forgiven you so much.

Then you are really rich, happy and proud of yourself.

Thank you for reading through to the end of this book.

I sincerely hope that you will achieve absolute success in the seven areas of your life.

P.S. My eczema is gone, my fast is broken, the book is finished and about my love life ... hmm... Let's talk about it in another book?

EPILOGUE: MY MESSAGE FOR YOU[22]

As I have told you, this double book is far from perfect, but I wanted to share with you what I have learned and applied so far.

This 12-day experience taught me one thing:
ANYTHING IS POSSIBLE TO THOSE WHO BELIEVE.

Here is my personal message for you:

You are born free: decide who you want to be, and what you want to accomplish. If you don't know what it is, search within yourself and find your deepest dreams, clarify them, quantify them, and make them come true.

Turn your passion into a profession, and achieve excellence in your field. You have been divinely created, you are unique and exceptional. Burst through your mental limits and create new things.

Keep it simple, don't have a plan B. Focus on one thing only. To decide is to dominate. Stick to your principles; a promise is hidden behind each one of them.

Act quickly and well, because it's the only way to move forward. Never do anything just for money, it's just one of your resources. The most precious resource is your time: your life on this Earth.

Give to your loved ones, give to your audience and give to those who have nothing. Persevere and finish your race, because at the finish line, victory awaits at the end.

Sincerely, Eric.

---

[22] Watch the video for Day 13: http://12days.co/13